_By_

On the Occasion of

Date

Presented to

(SECRETS OF)
CONFIDENCE

A 60-DAY DEVOTIONAL FOR THE INNER YOU

RAMONA RICHARDS

BARBOUR
PUBLISHING

Contents

INTRODUCTION

Every woman alive has felt hesitant and nervous at some point. We worry intensely about a variety of things from our families to our jobs, and while it is human nature to want to succeed, achieve, and triumph over obstacles, we live in a culture that tells us we should be able to do this out of our own talents and abilities. So when we fail, when we can't move forward on our own efforts, we feel defeated and hopeless.

The devotions in this book are designed to show women that the true source of confidence lies only with God. While our own strength will fail us, He never will. When terror overwhelms us, He is there, letting us know that He is greater than anything the world can throw at us.

There is an old hymn that tells us:

> *I sing because I'm happy,*
> *I sing because I'm free.*
> *His eye is on the sparrow,*
> *And I know He watches me.*

The God who sees every sparrow, the God who sent His Son to die for us, will give us hope and confidence to face anything.

CONFIDENCE IN ACTION

When Abigail saw David, she quickly got off her donkey and bowed down before David with her face to the ground. She fell at his feet and said: "My lord, let the blame be on me alone. Please let your servant speak to you; hear what your servant has to say."

1 SAMUEL 25:23–24 NIV

How many women have the confidence to believe they could stop an army?

Abigail of Maon, married to Nabal, lived in a culture in which women had little social or legal power. Her own talents would have been focused on her home, not the court or the battlefield. Yet, while Abigail would have been seen as little more than the wife of a fool by her society, she was far from powerless. Scripture describes her as intelligent and beautiful, and even her husband's servants relied on her wisdom when Nabal put the household at risk with his foolish pride.

The reason was that Abigail had a secret weapon: God. Faced with the news that an angry David was leading an equally enraged army toward her home, she didn't hesitate. Trusting in God's protection—and in her belief that David was indeed a man after God's own heart—she confronted the furious warrior and begged him to hear her. She appealed to his own belief in God's mercy and judgment, and she asked him to let God deal with Nabal.

Abigail had the intelligence and wisdom to know what to do, but her confidence to put her knowledge into action had only one source—the same source every believing woman can draw on. Standing on a mountain path, with only food-laden donkeys at her back, Abigail was at the complete mercy of David's rage. He could have killed her without question and gone on to slaughter her family and servants. As he most likely would have had she not had the courage to intervene.

Her belief in God, however, gave her the confidence to stand up in front of four hundred men and declare that letting God lead was a better path to follow.

The result must have astonished those men. David listened to this humble woman, overwhelmed by her confidence and wisdom. His rage vanished; he called her blessed. After Nabal died, David further rewarded her by making Abigail his wife.

No matter what our gifts and talents, they are made even more powerful when put into action under God's guidance. Trusting Him, believing in His power within us, gives all believers the confidence to take action.

COURAGE TO ENDURE

For examples of patience in suffering,
dear brothers and sisters, look at the prophets
who spoke in the name of the Lord.
We give great honor to those who
endure under suffering. Job is an example
of a man who endured patiently.
From his experience we see how the Lord's plan
finally ended in good, for he is full of
tenderness and mercy.

JAMES 5:10–11 NLT

From a very early age, Shelley Hendrix felt a call to share the Lord with those around her. She realized that her true value comes from a deep and abiding relationship with Christ, and the love with which God had filled her heart made her ache to help others, especially women and young girls, understand how their worth is centered in Him.

Shelley's path toward this goal, however, has not been an easy one. The trials that she experienced—that most of us experience sooner or later—shook her to the core. In her own words, she explains how the agonies of life threatened to shake her confidence in God and her own ministry, and how the words of James helped her look to the Bible for guidance—and role models.

"In my calling to be a woman of God, I often find myself struggling with the painful events that the Lord, in His goodness, allows to come into my life. There is so much temptation in those times to lose confidence in God and to turn to my own resources to make life unfold in a way that would be more pleasant for me. There are so many different forms of suffering in the life of a believer.

"Through the painful events in my life—divorce, miscarriages, relationship struggles, and simply living in a sin-cursed world—I have been able to maintain confidence in the Lord and in His working in my life as a result of the truths of who He is and who He says I am as His daughter. And because I am His child, all of His resources are available to me.

"He is good and He does good (see Psalm 119:68). I can trust in Him confidently because of His good character. And, looking back at Job and the other prophets, and even those believers whose names are not found in the pages of scripture, I can see in their lives 'the Lord's plan finally ended in good' and take as truth for myself that He has an end intended for my struggles and pain as well—that in my life He is 'full of tenderness and mercy.'

"How could I not trust Him?"

CONFIDENCE FROM
ENCOURAGING OTHERS

*"You yourself have done this plenty of times,
spoken words that clarify, encouraged those
who were about to quit. Your words have
put stumbling people on their feet,
put fresh hope in people
about to collapse."*

JOB 4:3–4 MSG

I don't think I can do this." Elaine sat in the car, refusing to get out. I struggled with what to say, saying a little prayer for guidance. "What are you afraid of?"

She shrugged. "I'm not sure it's fear. More like the embarrassment that makes you clean the house before the maid comes." She paused. "I feel like I should lose weight before joining a gym."

I almost laughed. Elaine had struggled with her weight for years, and here we were, about to go into a gym for the first time in more than twenty years. Elaine, however, now faced her fear of humiliation, in her words, "of being an old fat lady in front of all those young, hard bodies and skinny girls."

It seemed trivial to both of us, given the much larger issues in our lives. But Elaine's fear was real, and it threatened to be crippling, preventing her from making a much-needed change in her life. She needed encouragement; I wanted to offer to her the same help she'd so often given me in the past. It was then that this passage from Job came to mind, when Eliphaz reminded Job that he had so often encouraged his friends in the past, when their doubts had led them away from God.

His words had helped them stay on the right path.

"Do you remember," I asked Elaine, "telling me over and over that I'm beautiful in the eyes of God, no matter what people here think?"

She cut her gaze toward me. She didn't want to hear this.

I grinned. "Your advice has always helped me when I had problems thinking straight, especially about God. You are one of the most confident women I know, about everything but this. You told me that confidence lies in God. Yes?"

Reluctantly, Elaine nodded.

"So why is it you think He'll support you with your hardest tasks, but not give you the confidence to do something as simple as walking into a gym?"

We sat in the dark for a long time as Elaine stared out over the parking lot clustered with cars. "I guess," she said finally, "if He can help David and Job through their darkest times, He can help me face a few skinny girls."

We got out, thankful that God could give us the confidence to tackle any task, no matter how big—or small.

THE CONFIDENCE TO SAVE A CHILD

When she could no longer hide him,
she took an ark of bulrushes for him,
daubed it with asphalt and pitch,
put the child in it, and laid it in the reeds
by the river's bank.

EXODUS 2:3 NKJV

Imagine carrying a precious child within you for nine months, all the while knowing that if you gave birth to a boy, he would be immediately killed on orders from the government. Like every other Hebrew mother of her time, Jochebed knew that her newborn son, Moses, would be murdered if she didn't take drastic action.

For the first three months after his birth, Jochebed hid her squirmy child, but she knew she couldn't conceal him forever. So she did exactly as the pharaoh commanded: "Every son who is born you shall cast into the river" (Exodus 1:22 NKJV). Only this resourceful mother went one step further, encasing her child in bulrushes and pitch before slipping him into the water. On the bank, his sister kept a close watch over her tiny brother.

Few believers today can understand the risks and fears of living under the harsh conditions of the Hebrews under the pharaohs. Yet Jochebed, as a daughter of Levi and married to a man of her own tribe, must have known the promises of God. Choosing to follow her beliefs instead of the cruelty of her world, she stepped out in faith in an effort to protect her beautiful son. Her confidence in God allowed her to release Moses into the river, only to have him return to her arms as the protected grandson of the man who had wanted him dead. As a result, she delivered to the world one of its greatest leaders, and her entire family was blessed (see Numbers 26:59).

Although mothers today don't usually have to take such dire actions to protect our children, we are called upon to be advocates for them, to support and stand beside them, pray for them, and let them go when the time comes. All of which requires confidence in God's loving care and plan for our own lives—and that of each child born to us.

COURAGE TO CHANGE

Don't copy the behavior and customs of this world, but let God transform you into a new person by changing the way you think. Then you will know what God wants you to do, and you will know how good and pleasing and perfect his will really is.

ROMANS 12:2 NLT

As a motivational speaker, Tracy Hurst is a dynamic Bible teacher who uses humor and a down-to-earth personality to draw people to her message of the love and transforming power of Christ. As a Christian counselor and cohost of Moody Radio's "Marriage and Family Today" program, Tracy also works hard to help people call on the power of Christ to change their lives, to move away from the consequences of ill-made choices and into the life-altering light of God.

The success of Tracy's leadership comes, in part, because she has walked a few of those dark paths herself. She's been there. As a teenager, she was rebellious and angry. She fought a deep depression and even became suicidal.

Then, at sixteen, she accepted Christ, which began a life transformation so dynamic that her story began to inspire others around her. She became a teen leader in her school and community. She fought her school board so she could lead a Bible study at her high school, and she even led her own mother to the Lord. Her enthusiasm for the Lord continued as she went on to pursue both a bachelor's and master's degree in psychology.

She worked for New Life Clinics, and today she has a counseling practice at the AlphaCare Christian Counseling Center.

Yet none of this would have been possible if Tracy had not allowed Christ to change her life through scripture. She writes, "Romans 12:2 made it clear that I was not going to know His will for my life until I allowed God to change the way I think. I needed to make the Word of God the final authority in my life. I am now in His perfect will as a Christian counselor, and I have the privilege of sharing this truth with my clients."

This verse gave Tracy Hurst the courage to change her life, and as a result she has been able to reach out to people all over the world, helping them change as well.

God Hears You

And this is the confidence that we have in him,
that, if we ask any thing according to his will,
he heareth us: and if we know that he hear us,
whatsoever we ask, we know that we have
the petitions that we desired of him.

1 John 5:14–15 KJV

Maybe you're praying for the wrong thing." Marilee's gentle voice and soft tone let me know she didn't intend to be critical.

"What do you mean?" I asked. Since returning to our church following my divorce, Marilee had been a mentor and a good friend.

"Maybe it's not in His will for her to be healed."

Ah. Not an easy thing for a mother to hear. My daughter, her disabilities caused at birth by a lack of oxygen, grinned up at us from her bed. Marilee, her godmother and frequent caregiver, loved her almost as much as I did. For me, a desire for Rachel's healing grew directly from that love. Wouldn't God want the same thing?

"Maybe," answered Marilee, "but maybe not. After all, He looks at the heart, the mind, and the spirit. Not the body." She reminded me of this passage in 1 John. "Maybe He has a plan for her that doesn't involve walking around and going to school. Healing is your will for her, but it might not be His."

How frustrating! I chafed, rebelled, and argued with God for weeks about this. Then, one Sunday I observed Rachel through a glass panel in the nursery door. The church had placed a cot in the toddler's nursery so Rachel could lie down and watch her videos during church. The toddlers sat next to her, petting her, offering her toys. When I went in, they asked dozens of questions: "Why can't she walk? Why won't she answer me? What's wrong with her? Is she sick? Will she get better?"

That night, I went to my knees with a new prayer, asking this time for help in following His will: "Lord, she is Your child. Use her as You see fit. Just give me a clue on how to help You care for her."

That prayer has been answered in more ways than I can possibly count. Rachel's presence in our church brought greater awareness of persons with disabilities to the entire congregation. I've written and published a number of articles about Rachel's life and God's blessings on us both. I've spoken about her to church groups. While Rachel's health has been a furious roller-coaster ride, she has persevered. The doctors told me she might live until she was eight or nine.

She's now eighteen—and I'm still praying, with the full confidence that God's listening carefully.

TO INSTRUCT
THE ONES WE LOVE

She kissed them,
and they lifted up their voices and wept.
And they said to her,
"Surely we will return with you to your people."

RUTH 1:9–10 NKJV

Although believing women are encouraged to mentor other women (see Titus 2:3–5), there are few examples of women actually doing that in scripture. Naomi, however, mentored her daughter-in-law Ruth with love and respect as well as a touch of necessity.

A woman of great courage, Naomi left all that she knew twice in her life. First, when a famine struck Judah, she moved with her husband, Elimelech, and their two sons to Moab. They did well there, and after Elimelech died, her sons married Moabite women, Orpah and Ruth. The family thrived for the next ten years, until both sons died as well, leaving the three women widowed and desperate.

Weighing her choices, Naomi decided her best option lay with returning to her family in Judah. The famine had passed, and she had relatives who could help her. She encouraged Orpah and Ruth to return to their fathers' houses, where they could find warmth and support, as well.

Neither of the younger women wanted to go. What a testimony to the bonding love these women must have felt for each other! Finally Orpah relented and left, but Ruth stayed, pleading with her mother-in-law with some of the most beautiful words of commitment in history (see Ruth 1:16–17). Not only was Ruth willing to give up her friends, family, and home, she was also giving up her gods. She chose the Lord, turning her life to Him because of the work she'd seen Him do in the lives of Naomi and her family. Naomi led Ruth to God by just loving Him, worshiping Him, and relying on Him.

Naomi's mentoring of Ruth continued once they returned to Judah. Ruth, a stranger, knew nothing of the ways of her new land. Naomi guided her, told her exactly what to do, where to go, and what to say. Ruth trusted her and obediently did as her mother-in-law instructed. As a result, Naomi's kinsman Boaz took Ruth as his wife, and their son became an ancestor of Jesus Christ.

Mature believers know that one of the best ways to reach other people for the Lord is to let them see His work in their lives and how much they love Him. Although Naomi grieved over some of the events in her life, especially the loss of her husband and sons (see Ruth 1:20), she never gave up hope nor stopped loving and worshiping God.

GOD IS YOUR CONFIDENCE

*Do not be afraid of sudden terror, nor of trouble from
the wicked when it comes; for the LORD
will be your confidence, and will keep
your foot from being caught.*

PROVERBS 3:25–26 NKJV

The first thing Linda Evans Shepherd noticed as the shock of the accident wore off was the silence.

Her ears still rang from the shattering impact of the other vehicle hitting hers, and adrenaline still pumped through her veins. She was trembling but unhurt as she scrambled to pull herself away from the mangled car, one thought occupying her mind.

Why wasn't her daughter crying?

Eighteen-month-old Laura had been strapped securely in her car seat behind Linda, but the crash had severed her car, and Linda felt terror and panic surge through her as she twisted around. Laura was gone.

At that moment, Linda, a well-known Christian writer and speaker, faced the horror of a mother's worst nightmare. She scrambled through the wreckage, finally finding Laura, still in her seat, facedown on the pavement. The brain damage she sustained would leave her in a coma for eleven months. And, as Linda sat vigil by her daughter's bed, twenty-seven "experts" came and went, telling Linda that Laura would remain in a vegetative state for the rest of her life.

Linda, however, never gave up hope on

Laura—or God—no matter how much fear she felt for her child. She felt Him leading her as her daughter's advocate, and Linda's confidence in God's support and answered prayers gave her the strength to continue to push for care—and to believe.

While Laura's brain damage was permanent, her vegetative state was not. Today she is a glorious teenager who plays, communicates, and loves with a purity that makes her a living example of God's unconditional affection for all His children. As Linda writes, "Laura, like other disabled people, has a purpose. For it's not about ability, it's about love. Laura fulfills her purpose better than anyone I know." And Linda's faith-based confidence shines as proof of God's guidance through even the most mind-numbing fears.

GOD BUILDS YOU UP

*Perhaps you think we are saying all this just to
defend ourselves. That isn't it at all. We tell
you this as Christ's servants, and we know
that God is listening. Everything we
do, dear friends, is for your benefit.*

2 CORINTHIANS 12:19 NLT

You can do this. Take a deep breath— no, not that deep!"

The young woman in front of me was so nervous that her convention name tag quivered. "I don't think I'll get through it without throwing up on her shoes!"

We were both waiting for an appointment with an editor at a major publishing house. In less than ten minutes, we had to explain what our books were about and convince the editor that they would sell to readers. Writers make these kinds of pitches frequently, but each time, we almost feel as if our careers are on the line. The next ten minutes will make or break us.

I grabbed my friend's hand. "Listen to me. We practiced this. You know this story better than anyone and you love it. Tell it like you love it. Trust yourself. Trust your heart. Trust God."

She stared at me a moment, then nodded. "Pray with me."

In a lot of jobs, there is more competition than support. I've not found this to be true among writers, however, especially romance writers. They gather, support each other's efforts, hold workshops, share information about agents and publishers, and, best of all, praise each other. They build each other up.

This is what Paul was trying to do for the Corinthians in his second letter to them. Paul didn't write in order to bring attention to himself; instead, he used the authority God gave him to teach the Corinthians, to attempt to move them closer to Christ so they could grow in the faith.

God wants this for all of His children. He gave us His Word for our edification, as well as great teachers to help us grow and understand our faith and how it works in our everyday lives. He wants us to succeed, and He will send the right mentors and teachers to help us, just as he sent Paul to the Corinthians. With His support, we should have the confidence to step out toward whatever challenge awaits us.

To Follow God's Call

And Deborah, a prophetess, the wife of Lapidoth,
she judged Israel at that time.

JUDGES 4:4 KJV

Throughout scripture, the faith women have in God provides them with the confidence to stand up for their beliefs, face down armies, and deal with the pressures of their lives. One woman is even called to guide ten thousand men into battle.

The only woman to sit as a judge over Israel, Deborah's most vital relationships are introduced in this first mention of her. The prophets in Old Testament times were men and women called by God to communicate His will to the people. Thus, Deborah already had a strong relationship with the Lord when she was called to sit as judge for Israel at a time of harsh oppression. She was also a wife, with an established household and place in her world. Yet in a society that did not always value women as leaders, she answered God's call on her life.

Using her wisdom to settle disputes for her people, however, is a far cry from leading them into battle against an army featuring nine hundred iron chariots, vehicles that had revolutionized warfare and forced the Israelites to seek refuge in fortified cities. Jabin, the king in Canaan, had dealt harshly with the Israelites for more than twenty years, using his army to keep them under his rule. Finally, they cried out to God for relief in what appeared to be an impossible situation to overcome.

Deborah, however, had the ability to see beyond the current situation. She was a woman of vision, and she called on Barak to do as the Lord had commanded, to take his troops and prepare to face Sisera, Jabin's general, in a battle to save their people. Barak's response—that he would do so only if she was with him (see Judges 4:8)—underscores the trust Israel had placed in the woman God had called for them.

God always looks for women who are ready to embrace His vision for their lives, their family, and even their nation. Such women of vision have the courage that enables them to conquer and overcome in situations that would otherwise seem unconquerable.

CONFIDENCE AFTER LOSS

"And if I go and prepare a place for you,
I will come back and take you to be with
me that you also may be where I am."

JOHN 14:3 NIV

One of the most difficult challenges we face in this life is dealing with the loss of someone we love. It was this agony that plummeted writer and teacher Jennifer Stephens to an all-time spiritual low during the Christmas season of 2000.

Jennifer and her father had always had a special bond. When he died on December 23 after a brief illness, the shock of his sudden passing was magnified because she was four months pregnant with her first child—a child who would never know the special man who would have been her grandfather.

For Jennifer, the loss left a huge, gaping hole in her life. She had never imagined life without her father. Now he was gone, forever out of her life, and she grieved that her unborn child would never have the chance to have a special relationship with him. Jennifer had seen her father interact many times with her nephew, and she knew what a wonderful grandpa he was. She had desperately wanted that for her baby as well. Life went on, however, and Jennifer muddled through the next few months feeling lonelier and lonelier even though her husband remained close, reaching out to her.

Then on June 28, 2001, after twenty-two hours of labor, Jennifer gave birth to her daughter. Yet the joy she and her husband felt was tempered when, only an hour later, they discovered that their beautiful child had a cleft palate. While not a life-threatening illness, it was still an unexpected challenge for the new parents, and more than ever, Jennifer missed her dad.

As the new parent of a child with a special need, she needed his counsel, his parenting wisdom. Looking for that comfort, she turned to her Bible, opening it to a bookmarked passage that had been read at her dad's funeral: "And if I go and prepare a place for you. . ."

With a sudden sense of peace, Jennifer realized that her dad had just gone on ahead of her, getting things ready for when she will go home to her Father's house. One day she will be with her father again. One day Jesus and her dad will come for her and they will take her home to the place prepared just for her. This knowledge gave Jennifer the courage and the confidence to go forward, sharing with her daughter the memories and the faith of a special man.

GOD REJOICES IN YOUR CONFIDENCE

*I rejoice therefore that I have
confidence in you in all things.*

2 CORINTHIANS 7:16 KJV

B ut God wants you to have confidence!"

Those words echoed in my head as I tried not to hyperventilate. Stage fright was making my palms sweat and my knees quiver. Waiting to be introduced, I fought to stay calm, remembering those words of support from a woman in my church. I loved Ann dearly, and she had been a spiritual mentor—and mother—to me. When I'd been invited to speak for the first time at a church, I had sought her out.

"I don't know if I can do this. Even the thought of standing in front of all those people does all kinds of weird stuff to my body."

Ann laughed. "But this is a gift, an opportunity from God to give your testimony, to tell those folks what He's done in your life. You can't turn your back on that."

"What kind of testimony will it be if I make a fool out of myself?"

"You won't. Pray about it. He gave you the story, led you to live it. He'll certainly give you the confidence to share it. Remember what Paul wrote to the Corinthians, once they'd straightened themselves out and were back on the right road. They'd gained confidence in their faith, and Paul rejoiced in that." She hugged me. "God wants you to be confident!"

I took another deep breath and let it out slowly as I heard the hostess winding up her introduction. "Okay, God," I whispered, "let's get me through this, and we'll both rejoice." I stepped up, thanked the hostess, and gripped the sides of the podium as if it were going to flee from the room. My voice trembled, but as my message began to flow, I relaxed.

God got me through it, of course, that day and many times since, mostly because Ann's words made an impact that has never lessened. God wants us to be confident—in our faith, in our gifts, and especially in Him, and He rejoices when our trust in Him gives us the confidence to tackle whatever challenge He puts before us.

CLAIMING GOD'S PROMISE

And the LORD spake unto Moses, saying,
The daughters of Zelophehad speak right: thou
shalt surely give them a possession of an
inheritance among their father's brethren;
and thou shalt cause the inheritance of
their father to pass unto them.

NUMBERS 27:6–7 KJV

What astonishing confidence the five daughters of Zelophehad had in God's provisions for women! Imagine the courage required for Mahlah, Noah, Hoglah, Milcah, and Tirzah to stand up before their entire community and ask their leaders to deviate from the established legal tradition as they petitioned: "Why should the name of our father be removed from among his family because he had no son? Give us a possession among our father's brothers" (Numbers 27:4 NKJV).

The laws God gave to the Hebrews following the Exodus were essential in not only maintaining law and order in the community but the property rights for each individual. This was crucial in ensuring that a family endured and prospered. Normally, such property passed through the sons. But what happened if there were no sons?

Zelophehad was a descendant of Joseph, making his lineage vital to the community. While he died without sons, he did leave behind five daughters. According to the existing law, Zelophehad's possessions were to pass to his brothers. Instead, these five women stepped out in faith and appealed to Moses so that their father's name and lineage could continue.

When Moses then turned to God for an answer, the Lord agreed with the daughters of Zelophehad, then went a step further: "If a man dies and has no son, then you shall cause his inheritance to pass to his daughter" (Numbers 27:8). Only if a man had no children at all would his brothers inherit. In a patriarchal society in which women had few rights, this was a radical change. Far from being a minor legal matter that was resolved in a few moments, this God-dictated shift in Hebrew law reveals exactly how much He cares for women.

OVERCOMING FEAR
WITH LOVE

For God has not given us a spirit of fear,
but of power and of love and of a sound mind.

2 TIMOTHY 1:7 NKJV

M rs. Eckles," the court clerk said, "we're ready for you."

These simple words changed Jan Eckles's life forever. Yet, she had almost let fear keep her from hearing them.

Most people are a bit nervous when starting a job, but Jan Eckles faced a few more obstacles than the average new employee. As an adult, a hereditary retinal disease had left her blind, and she had only recently learned to move about the city with a cane. She was also entering a brand-new field, that of court interpreter.

On that first day, an almost overwhelming sense of apprehension gripped Jan as she waited outside the courtroom. A sudden and sobering reality surged through her, making her feel inadequate with both her lack of experience as a Spanish interpreter and her limited knowledge of legal terminology. She was almost ready to back out when the court clerk came for her. Jan followed the clerk in, and with trembling hands and cramping stomach, she prepared for the frightening unknown.

That's when the promise Paul had written to Timothy rang in her ears: "For God has not given us a spirit of fear. . . ."

The session began. She concentrated so intensely on each utterance that the pounding of the judge's gavel startled her. After ordering a recess, he asked Jan to approach the bench.

Painfully aware of her deficient abilities, Jan took a deep breath in preparation to receive a well-deserved reprimand. What she heard instead surprised her as much as the pounding gavel.

"Mrs. Eckles, I'm bilingual, as well," the judge said with a tender voice, "and I'm very impressed with the accuracy level of your interpretation and your professionalism."

With those words, Jan's new career took flight, and she heard in them not only the pleasure of the judge but the reassurance of God, as if He were reminding her, "If you trust in Me, the results exceed all your expectations."

CONFIDENCE TO SPEAK THE WORD

"Now, Lord, look on their threats,
and grant to Your servants that with
all boldness they may speak Your word,
by stretching out Your hand to heal, and
that signs and wonders may be done through
the name of Your holy Servant Jesus."
And when they had prayed,
the place where they were assembled together
was shaken; and they were all filled
with the Holy Spirit, and they spoke
the word of God with boldness.

ACTS 4:29–31 NKJV

Evangelism is not one of my gifts. I've known that for a long time. God has blessed me many times over in my life: I'm a writer, a teacher, sometimes a speaker. I have a child who is the light of my life and friends whose support never wavers. The joy that being a woman of Christ has brought me seems endless. Yet speaking about those blessings has never been easy for me, and I've often prayed for confidence with this, especially where those friends are concerned.

Because of my background and various interests, many of my friends are not Christian. Some of them live rather wild, undisciplined—and often lost—lives. They know I'm a Christian, and they respect that. Yet I'm well aware that they don't want to hear about God and His Son.

When I found this passage, I turned instead to prayer: *Give me the strength to speak of You, Lord—and even more, the right doors.*

The answer I received over and over to this prayer has been: Live it. Instead of preaching or witnessing, just be the best Christian I know how. When I do, my friends begin to feel more comfortable asking me questions about my faith. When God moved the heart of a woman

I'd known for more than ten years, she called me with questions about scripture and the ways God moves in our lives. Today she's an active member of a local church and a firm believer that she is where God wants her to be.

Not long after she joined the church, my phone rang late one night, just as I was preparing for bed. A mutual friend, witnessing the changes he'd seen in our friend, had some questions about Jesus Christ. We talked until after two in the morning.

Perhaps I'm never meant to reach thousands with my words or speak to hundreds about my faith. But through this prayer in Acts, I've found the confidence to reach out with my faith, one friend at a time.

THE CONFIDENCE TO RISK EVERYTHING

So they went, and came to the house
of a harlot named Rahab,
and lodged there. . . .
Then the woman took the two men
and hid them.

JOSHUA 2:1, 4 NKJV

Any woman who thinks she needs to perfect her life or faith before serving the Lord should take another look at Rahab. One of the women named in the record of faithful heroes (see Hebrews 11:31), Rahab's early life hardly appeared to be a model-perfect picture of morality and belief. Her growing faith in the works of the Lord, however, gave her the confidence to put everything she knew at risk.

Rahab's life could not have been easy. The text refers to her as a prostitute, although some archaeological evidence indicates Rahab may have operated an inn, since the two jobs were often closely linked and scripture says that the spies lodged with her. Either way, her profession was difficult and dangerous. Yet Rahab met a lot of travelers, and she had learned in great detail what was going on in her city as well as her country. Thus, while Rahab's decision to hide the Hebrew spies on her roof may seem a bit impulsive as first told in Joshua 2, she later makes it clear that this is something she'd been thinking about for some time.

When ordered by the king to surrender the spies, she quickly hid the men on the roof and covered them with flax. She then explained to the king's messenger that the spies had already departed, risking a charge of treason. After the king's men left, however, Rahab confronted the two Israelis about what the Lord had been doing and asked for their help (see Joshua 2:8–13). She had been listening to her clients and marveling at all the Lord had done in Canaan. Although other citizens of Jericho probably knew as much as she did about the conquests of Israel, this quick-thinking and intelligent woman was the only one to put more faith in God than the fortifications of her city. Believing instead that Jericho would never stand against the power of God, Rahab chose to follow the Lord, no matter what the cost.

Her faith saved her family—and this strong woman became one of the ancestors of Jesus Christ. Her example reminds us today that no matter what our background or circumstances, what God wants most of all is simply our trust and love.

COURAGE TO FACE THE DARKNESS

*Your word is a lamp to my feet
and a light to my path.*

PSALM 119:105 NKJV

When Jan Eckles was thirteen, she was diagnosed with symptoms of Retinitis Pigmentosa (RP). This hereditary disease affects the retina of the eye, causing it to deteriorate slowly. The ophthalmologist she saw at the time, however, told her she would probably see no significant changes until she was sixty or older.

Jan was stunned at age twenty-seven, then, when a doctor told her she should no longer drive a car. Pregnant with her second child, her first reactions were anger—and denial. Jan continued to drive for another five years, until she lost so much of her peripheral vision that she finally realized she was putting herself and her children in danger. Ultimately, her vision closed in completely, leaving her devastated. She writes of the experience:

"When a black curtain fell on my world, its darkness swallowed my dreams of a life of fulfillment and joy. I refused to face this reality, but the hereditary retinal disease forced me through the seasons of painful adjustments. The spring of hope as I desperately looked for treatments, transplants, medications, or vitamins. But the summer's hot rays of disappointments scorched all hope for a cure. The fall brought unavoidable changes—in my plans, my dreams, and activities. And finally the winter with its cold and cruel sentence to a dark prison labeled 'blind for life.' My emotional world darkened as well with the desperate longing to have my life normal as before. My blindness robbed my sons of a mom who could care for them. I anguished knowing my husband no longer had a wife who could do her part for the family. I prayed feverishly, 'Lord, what will I do? How can I make my life worthwhile. . .help me to go on. . .to survive in a sighted world.' "

Jan was ready to give up, but God was not ready to give up on her. When she was at her lowest, that's when God came into her heart, reminding her that spiritual illumination has an eternal, never-failing source to light her path. That "light" gave her the strength and courage to face her blindness, adapt, and move on to a much brighter future.

Her physical surroundings remain in the dark, but her life now shines under the light of God's Word. Our lives can, too—when we put our trust in God.

You Will Walk
the Highest Hills

The Sovereign LORD is my strength;
he makes my feet like the feet of a deer,
he enables me to go on the heights.

HABAKKUK 3:19 NIV

The sun rose, although I barely noticed. I had slept little, and my body felt numb. I knew that physically I was all right. Yet my world had closed in with a darkness that had left me remote from any feelings. Emotions of any kind—anger, love, even self-pity—seemed like foreign concepts to my mind, which was devoid of most thought. Even the slightest movement appeared to be impossible.

In the distance, I could hear my daughter stirring in her bed. She would soon need breakfast and a diaper change. Responsibility beckoned. *I have to get up,* I told myself, and almost as a last straw, I prayed for help.

For no apparent reason, my mind then flashed to the phrase "hind's feet in high places."

I knew it well. Habakkuk's hymn of faith is one of the most beautiful passages in the Bible. He was looking back on the destruction of the land and the people of Israel caused by the Babylonian invasion. This bleak time was one of hopelessness and depression, a time when many could have easily walked away from their faith and their God. The prophet, however, put things in perspective, reminding us all that no matter how bad things get, God is always in control, always ready to help and aid us.

As someone who deals with stark cycles of depression, I had relied on these verses before. On days when simply getting out of bed to care for my daughter requires a proactive and determined effort, I find trusting that God will lift me again to be one of the more encouraging aspects of my life.

Because He has lifted me, and I have stood on those high places. I cherish those memories, and I hold them as reminders that no matter how bad the darkness is today, next month or next year will be different, better, lighter.

For me, these lovely verses are not simply words of love and understanding. They are also cherished words of hope.

TO FOLLOW THOSE WHO TEACH US

But Ruth said, "Do not urge me to leave you or
turn back from following you; for where you go,
I will go, and where you lodge, I will lodge.
Your people shall be my people,
and your God, my God."

RUTH 1:16 NASB

Ruth must have been frightened almost out of her mind. With the loss of both her husband and brother-in-law, and the death of her father-in-law years earlier, Ruth's future was shaky and uncertain at best. Tradition said she should return to her parents' home, but Ruth and her sister-in-law, Orpah, clustered around Naomi, the grieving mother of their husbands. Ruth didn't want to return to the house of her father, but three widows alone had no way of supporting themselves.

Then Ruth's beloved mother-in-law, Naomi, decided to return to Judah. During her short marriage, Ruth had grown to admire and cherish the older woman, watching how she had nurtured her family and worshiped her God. Naomi had family in Judah who could take care of her, and as she prepared to make the move, Ruth and Orpah faced a gut-wrenching decision.

Although Orpah loved Naomi, she apparently recognized the wisdom in Naomi's advice, "Return, my daughters. Why should you go with me?" (Ruth 1:11 NASB). Ruth, however, had a dilemma that went far beyond financial and emotional support. Her closeness to Naomi, and the spiritual devotion of their home, had led Ruth to love the Lord. Thus, when she pledged her loyalty to Naomi, her words were not only of love for the woman and her people but for the God of all things (see Ruth 1:16). Ruth chose to trust God as well as the wisdom of Naomi. She placed herself in their care, and when Naomi gave her instructions on how to win the affection of Boaz, Ruth followed her guidance carefully. Her trust resulted in a secure home and family, and an honored place in the genealogy of Christ.

As women, we all benefit from the wisdom of our sisters in the faith, who can direct us and hold us accountable. Trusting God and choosing a wise mentor can help us as we learn more about our faith and develop a deeper and lasting relationship with our Lord.

CONFIDENCE TO SEE JUSTICE DONE

*Do what is good and run from evil—that you may live! Then the L*ORD *God Almighty will truly be your helper, just as you have claimed he is. Hate evil and love what is good; remodel your courts into true halls of justice.*

AMOS 5:14–15 NLT

This passage of scripture literally changed two women's lives for the better.

For several years, Ellen watched a situation in her own neighborhood grow increasingly unjust. A man who lived a few doors down brought a wife, Angela, to America from another country, mostly for the purpose of having children. Uncertain of American ways and unable to speak English, this young woman relied on her husband for everything. He controlled the money and all her social contacts. Ellen's first attempts at friendship with Angela were met with distrust and withdrawal.

As the couple's children started school, however, they brought home school papers, from which Angela learned basic English. She read more magazines and, finally, returned Ellen's efforts at friendship. This open door, however, brought Ellen more grief when she realized the severe level of physical and emotional abuse that the husband inflicted on his wife. She advised Angela to get help, but the young immigrant waited too long. The marriage exploded, landing the husband and wife in court. Angela, suddenly homeless, jobless, and still unable to speak a great deal of English, lost her beloved children because she could not adequately explain what had been happening in the home.

Like many of us, Ellen had been hesitant about how much to interfere in the personal business of another family. After seeking guidance through scripture and prayer, however, Ellen knew she had to speak up, not only for Angela but also for her children. Ellen and another friend stepped in and helped Angela find a lawyer, a place to live, and a job. They worked on improving Angela's English and wrote endless e-mails to the lawyer and the guardian ad litem who worked on the case. Ellen opened her home for extended visits with the children and took detailed notes anytime they spoke of their father's abuse.

"I couldn't let this go on and remain silent," Ellen said. "God simply spoke to my heart, and any hesitancy that I should help Angela fight for her children vanished."

Sometimes, even when we see an injustice, we don't think we have the skills or the strength to act. God, however, does have that strength, and He can provide the confidence and the wisdom to move forward.

GOD REWARDS CONFIDENCE

Do not throw away this confident trust
in the Lord, no matter what happens.
Remember the great reward it brings you!
Patient endurance is what you need now,
so you will continue to do God's will.
Then you will receive all that he has promised.

HEBREWS 10:35–36 NLT

I just don't understand how you could go see that movie!"

I heard that a lot in 2004, the year *The Passion of the Christ* hit theaters all over the world. I have many friends who are not believers, and some refused to face the violent depiction of the crucifixion. I had all the negative reviews waved in my face. One friend who went with me couldn't handle the violence and walked out early.

It was definitely not an easy film to watch. Even harder to face was the knowledge that Christ had the power to stop what was happening to Him at any moment. The film became, for me, an extremely emotional reminder of what Christ endured to follow His Father's will. To save God's children. To save me.

Yet it also underscored that many of Christ's disciples also suffered in His name. Being a believer, a devout follower of Jesus, has never been simple or easy. Believers have been ridiculed, often persecuted, just for holding on to their faith. As I watched the trial of Jesus on the screen, I couldn't help remembering what the scriptures say about the persecution of disciples like Peter, Stephen, Paul, and others. Throughout history, men and women have been tortured and killed for pursuing a faith in Jesus, and today there are still places in the world where being a Christian can mean risking life and limb.

Even when there's freedom to worship, temptations lie around every corner—sometimes even from those who care about us. As a single woman, for instance, I'm often asked about my choice of chastity in the face of days of loneliness, and sometimes ridiculed for it. While they are not physically torturous or life threatening, such attitudes still test us and call our faith into question.

Sometimes I've wavered; I'm human. But my confidence to continue on this path, the journey all believers make, comes from knowing how much God suffered for me, how much He loves me and wants me to succeed, and the knowledge that the reward waiting at the end is more precious than I can imagine.

CONFIDENCE TO
TAKE A STAND

*"For if you remain completely silent at this time,
relief and deliverance will arise for the Jews
from another place, but you and your father's house
will perish. Yet who knows whether
you have come to the kingdom for such
a time as this?"*

ESTHER 4:14 NKJV

Few women in the world have ever been as blessed as Esther. Although she lost her parents at a young age, she had a loving family and a caring and wise mentor in Mordecai. She had great beauty and a gentle heart. People were drawn to her and cared about her. When she was brought to the palace for a year of beauty treatments before being presented to the king, she quickly won the affection of the custodian of women, Hegai.

Yet one of the most striking characteristics about Esther was her absolute assurance of God's will for her life.

When Mordecai discovered the plot Haman had devised to execute every Jew, his first response was grief. He put on sackcloth and ashes and mourned with loud cries in the middle of the city. Esther, carefully cloistered within the palace, immediately sent to find out why. When Mordecai explained and asked her to plead their case with the king, Esther's first response was a natural, human fear.

She had good reason to be afraid of her husband. Throughout history, Ahasuerus had committed acts that made him appear a little unstable, including once commanding his sailors to whip uncooperative waves. The king had not called on her in more than a month, and a standing order gave him the right to execute anyone who came into his royal presence without being summoned.

Mordecai's response, however, reminded Esther that God had assured Abraham that the Jews would survive; help would come from somewhere, no matter what Esther did. Yet God's blessings on her might be a part of His plan for her life—and His plan to save His children.

Recognizing this wisdom, Esther asked that there be three days of fasting, after which she would approach the king. Her statement, "If I perish, I perish," is less a fatalistic acceptance than a solid assurance that God's plan for her life would play out as He intended. When Ahasuerus extended his scepter to welcome her, she knew that she had, in fact, come to the palace for just this moment.

While few women risk death these days, following God's relentless call on our lives can leave us facing situations completely out of our "comfort zone." Esther's story reminds us that God always has a plan in mind for us, and we can have confidence in knowing that we, too, are in His everlasting care.

GOD WILL NEVER LEAVE YOU

"For the LORD your God, He is the One who goes with you. He will not leave you nor forsake you."

DEUTERONOMY 31:6 NKJV

When Jan Eckles lost her eyesight in her early thirties, she struggled to find her center, emotionally and spiritually. She increasingly focused on the disease that had rendered her blind and her attempts to cope with her new world. She struggled with her own needs and wound up neglecting her family—especially her young husband.

"I need to talk to you," announced her husband one evening, in a cold and distant way that startled and frightened Jan. Immediately she knew that something was wrong, but she felt sure that whatever it was, they could it work out.

They left in the car so that their three boys couldn't hear the conversation, but even before they had left the neighborhood, her husband pronounced the words that forcefully punctured Jan's heart. His disappointment in their marriage, and her lack of attention, had caused him to look elsewhere for reassurance and comfort.

They were the words that no wife wants to hear. Jan's mouth went dry, and her stomach cramped. Shock turned to anger, then to rage, and finally to despair as she saw her marriage, her life, her whole world crumbling around her. She had dozens of questions, but the first two showed how much she really did care about her family: "What are we going to do?" and "What about the children?"

Her husband tried to answer, but Jan only felt herself sinking further into hopelessness.

Hope and a solution, however, were not far away. Jan prayed, remembering one of God's greatest promises to His children. She writes, "God's message brought sense and clarity to my confusion: 'I will never forsake you; I will never abandon you.' This trustworthy promise became the answer, the solution, the way out of my dark prison. My husband's rejection screamed 'abandonment, rejection, worthlessness.' But His Word reassured me—with or without a husband—I'd never be alone. God would be by my side.

"Equipped with confidence found in God, I informed my husband I'd be willing to let him go. But if he decided to stay, I would agree but only with specific conditions—our marriage would not be just the two of us; God would have to be at the center.

"He agreed. Thirty years later, with God as our guide and provider, we're more in love now than ever before."

God Gives You Wisdom

If any of you need wisdom, you should ask God, and it will be given to you. God is generous and won't correct you for asking.

James 1:5 cev

The older I've gotten, the more I've heard myself uttering the words, "Well, as my mother used to say. . ." It's almost become a joke among my friends, and they'll start to grin even before I can get some pithy proverb out. In fact, some of my mother's sayings are quite humorous, filled with homespun advice and earthy metaphors, like the day she was canning some beans and told me she was "hotter than a tent preacher in July." We're from Alabama, and I can assure you that camp meetings in the summer can get pretty hot!

It's not just the down-to-earth proverbs, however, that I depend on. My mother's wisdom sometimes amazes me. I began to ask her advice on people and situations when I was still just a kid, and she has seldom steered me wrong. When a kid was trying to bully me in junior high school, her advice helped me ease the situation in just a few days. When dealing with a variety of men in college had me spinning in confusion, she helped me find my feet again. She taught me how to handle money, work, even my faith.

I once asked her about the source of her wisdom, and she responded, "A little bit of living and a whole lot of prayer."

My mother had learned to rely on God for guidance and inspiration, which had made her invaluable to her friends and family. Even the tiniest problems were turned over to God, which gave her the confidence to help out those who came to her for advice.

I think it's very revealing that wisdom in scripture is portrayed as a woman (see Proverbs 1:20–21), since women seem to have an instinctual sense of how to take the little lessons of life and scripture and use them to nurture those they love. Even more encouraging is this reminder from James, that if we ever feel we're lacking in wisdom, all we have to do is ask—and God will provide both wisdom and the confidence to use it.

COURAGE TO
REST AND RENEW

*To whom He said,
"This is the rest with which you
may cause the weary to rest,"
and, "This is the refreshing."*

ISAIAH 28:12 NKJV

L ike many women in ministry, Eva Marie Everson seems to be always on the go. She travels extensively and speaks to more than fifty groups a year. She's a published author who has to balance writing deadlines with demands on her time from conferences, leadership responsibilities—and her family. Someone always wants something from her, and—like women in every walk of life—she has a hard time saying "No!"

For many women, this is a chronic problem. Being constantly busy becomes a way of life as we try to balance work and worship, fun and family, in an unending rush from one meeting to another, one soccer game to the next. Such a schedule eventually takes its toll, especially when the unexpected happens—a death, financial loss, or family upheaval.

Eva found out in a stark way when she finally found herself completely drained, physically, spiritually, and emotionally. It was a time of great trial in her life, and her friends had all but abandoned her. She was exhausted and lonely. That's when God gave her this scripture from Isaiah, reminding her that all His children are called to periods of rest and renewal.

The message is simple: We cannot be our best for Him if we are exhausted and drained of emotional, spiritual, and physical energy.

Her solution? "I went away for a long weekend and literally slept the whole time, waking only to the sweet 'whispers' of His Spirit to my soul. What He said to me. . .and taught me. . . in those hours were among the richest blessings of my life."

Eva returned to face everything she'd left behind for that weekend, but her time of rest and her renewed spirit gave her the resources to handle them calmly and with more creative solutions than she'd been able to find before.

God cares for us intimately, and He will always provide whatever it takes to be our best for Him, even if that need is nothing more than rest for our mind, body, and soul.

GOD IS YOUR ROCK AND FOUNDATION

My soul, wait silently for God alone,
For my expectation is from Him.
He only is my rock and my salvation;
He is my defense; I shall not be moved.
In God is my salvation and my glory;
The rock of my strength, and my refuge, is in God.

PSALM 62:5–7 NKJV

I looked out over the rolling ground around me, and a slow sense of panic seeped into my mind. The rock on which I perched was hardly a refuge, much less a fortress. My strength was waning, as was my last bit of hope.

"Why?" My voice echoed in the silence around me. "Why did you decide to go camping in January?" Snow and clumps of ice covered the ground near me, and the only sounds I could hear were the squirrels in the trees and the winds rustling through what was left of the leaves.

Lost. I didn't even want to say the word, but I had to. The day before, I had slipped on the ice and broken my ankle. The group I was with had been supportive, and my friend Sam had taken over my backpack. The night had been a miserable one of pain and despair. This morning, not wanting to slow the group down, I had left them early, hobbling back toward our cars as they broke camp. Only I had taken the wrong trail, one that had dwindled to a dead end. Trying to find my way back, I had even lost that trail completely, starkly aware that since Sam still had my pack, I had no food or supplies.

I had never felt so alone.

"Okay, God," I said aloud. "It's just You and me! And, boy, do I need Your help." I started to pray, but what came out of my mouth was not "Our Father. . ." Instead, it was the hymn we had sung last week in church, a song based on Psalm 62: "God is my refuge and my strength."

A sudden sense of peace flooded over me, and my heart stopped racing. As I relaxed, my head cleared of the panic, and I knew what I had to do.

Get up. Make some noise. I knew I had come from the west, so I pushed up and hobbled ten steps in that direction, and called out. Nothing. Ten more. Then another ten. Finally, after an hour, I heard someone call back. Two experienced campers from my group had made the same mistake, taken the same trail. Only they knew the way out, and had started to move away from me when they heard me call.

They led me out of the physical wilderness. My seeking God in that moment of panic, however, led me out of a spiritual wilderness, leaving me confident that I could do what had to be done.

THE CONFIDENCE TO HAVE UNWAVERING FAITH

*For she said to herself, "If only I may touch
His garment, I shall be made well."
But Jesus turned around, and when He saw her
He said, "Be of good cheer, daughter;
your faith has made you well."
And the woman was made
well from that hour.*

MATTHEW 9:21–22 NKJV

Twelve years. For twelve long years, this woman had bled, in more ways than just physically. Her illness rendered her "unclean" by Jewish standards, and her family and friends would have most likely ostracized her. If she were married, her husband wouldn't be allowed to touch her. The doctors she had sought out had taken her savings, leaving her needy, hopeless, and desperate (see Luke 8:43).

Then she heard about Jesus. She heard about the healings He had performed, knew that He spoke the word of God. Finally, there was hope. If only she could get to Him! Taking a chance, she pushed through the crowd, firmly believing that if she could touch the mere hem of His garment, she could be healed.

Luke also wrote of this moment, saying that Jesus immediately knew that power had gone out of Him and He turned, saying, "Who touched Me?" (Luke 8:45). The disciples were astonished. With all the people pushing and shoving at Him, how could He possibly distinguish one touch from another?

He knew, however, as did the woman, who was now terrified. She was unclean and she had dared touch a rabbi. She fell to her knees before Him, trembling, as she explained why she had reached out to Him.

Jesus' response, however, was one of compassion and assurance. He was impressed with the simple clarity of her faith, and He comforted her and declared her healed.

Although Jewish society at the time did not always value women, Jesus did. He reached out to them, befriended and healed them, and honored them in His ministry. Nothing has changed; Jesus still cherishes each one of us. Although trials and illness are a part of being human, our faith can remain strong in light of His love.

CONFIDENCE FROM
INNER PEACE

Be anxious for nothing, but in everything by prayer
and supplication, with thanksgiving,
let your requests be made known to God;
and the peace of God, which surpasses
all understanding, will guard your hearts
and minds through Christ Jesus.

PHILIPPIANS 4:6–7 NKJV

As a child, author Connie Neumann was painfully shy. As she grew up, she slowly became more comfortable with small groups of people, but the idea of speaking before a large group sent her diving for cover. So when she was asked to go from leading a small group of girls to becoming an AWANA director—which meant speaking to thirty-five elementary kids every week—she mumbled, "Let me pray about it."

AWANA stands for Approved Workmen Are Not Ashamed and is a type of scouting for Christians. Instead of earning patches and awards for knot tying or other wilderness skills, members get awards, patches, and pins for achievements like learning memory verses. Connie and her husband had been with the program for several years and were proud of the work they were doing. Connie, however, still wasn't convinced she was cut out to be a director.

She went home and, like Moses, prayed, "Lord, here am I. Send somebody else, anybody else, because I can't do this." But God's still small voice reminded her that with His strength she could find the peace to move forward with this call on her life.

Finally, she accepted and every Sunday afternoon, she'd clutch her churning stomach, muttering, "Lord, I can't do this. Help me."

Connie kept going, slowly finding an inner peace about her work as AWANA director. Two months later, another leader remarked to her, "You know, you're getting much better at this. Your voice doesn't shake nearly as much as it used to."

She laughed, but she heard the truth in those words. When she conquered the fear enough to stop thinking about her own nervousness, she started connecting with the kids. Seeing them begin to understand God's truth helped her turn dread into peace—and excitement about the children's learning.

More importantly, that training in AWANA prepared Connie to start and lead the praise team, youth choir, and drama program at her family's church, and eventually to speak at the regional AWANA leadership conferences. Last fall she even did a workshop called "Leadership for Introverts" that was very well received by the other shy people who attended.

God took that small first step and used it to prepare Connie for things she could never have imagined. She writes, "If anyone had told me even seven years ago that I'd ever willingly stand up in front of a crowd, I'd have laughed myself silly. But looking back, I can see how He used that small, scary beginning. With God's help and peace, I really can do whatever He asks."

THE CONFIDENCE TO BE USED BY GOD

And Mary said:
"My soul glorifies the Lord and my spirit
rejoices in God my Savior, for he has been
mindful of the humble state of his servant.
From now on all generations will call
me blessed."

LUKE 1:46–48 NIV

What if Mary had said no?

She could have. God didn't make her accept His will for her life; He let her choose.

As overwhelming as the appearance of an angel in her room must have been, Mary's choice should not have been an easy one. Her life was simple and stable: She was young, engaged to a good man, and ready to start her own home. Accepting God's will for her meant risking all of that, and much more. A woman who became pregnant during her betrothal could be accused of adultery and stoned. At the very least, Joseph would know that the child was not his and break off his commitment to her. If she survived, her life would be ruined.

Mary's mind, however, was on the Lord, not human society. She stood in awe of such an honor, and asked only how God planned to achieve this miracle. When she sang her praises of the Lord later (see Luke 1:46–55), this young girl expressed her joy and pride in being chosen by God. Her love of God and understanding of scriptures gave her complete confidence in her unhesitant "Yes, Lord!"

Mary was indeed blessed, but being Jesus'

mother also came with tremendous anxiety and heartache. She saw the glory of His miracles but also felt the pain of His death. Like any mother, she panicked when He went missing and rejoiced in His triumphs. And, after His death, she joined His disciples in the upper room (see Acts 1:12–14) to pray, grieve, and be with those who loved Him.

Mary could have said no, the same as any of us who feel God's tug on our lives. As Mary discovered, following God can lead us down a path filled with great pain as well as tremendous joy. Yet if we love Him and understand His love for us, then we will discover the confidence to say "yes!"

ANYTHING IS POSSIBLE

I can do all things through Christ
who strengthens me.

PHILIPPIANS 4:13 NKJV

Every successful effort begins with a first attempt—and the belief that you can succeed. The belief is one of the battle cries of motivational speaker and author Carol Grace Anderson, who today travels around the world, speaking to hundreds of groups, encouraging every person she meets to say, "Yes, I can!"

Yet this was not an easy lesson for Carol Grace. Born into a family of preachers, she heard so many sermons and so much scripture as a child that it all ran together, in one ear and out the other. As a teenager, she turned her back on it, and for years went her own way, following whatever message crossed her path. Only when she matured and became an independent-thinking adult did she begin to see the great value in the powerful teachings in the Bible.

One of those teachings was found in Philippians 4:13. Time and again, as Carol Grace faced the challenges we all do sooner or later, this verse gave her the strength to persevere. Then, when she was in her forties, Carol Grace discovered a new challenge in front of her, one put on her heart by the Lord: to become a professional speaker and author. Yet the thought of making such a drastic midlife career change left her uncertain where to turn. "I had no idea where to start," she writes. "I just had an inner feeling that God wanted me to pursue that path. And yet that verse kept weaving into my thoughts. Especially the first two words: I can."

So Carol Grace set out to learn a new way of life. It was a hard journey to become successful and sometimes it's still a challenge, but she's now grateful that she sliced through fear and took the risk. And whenever she needs renewed confidence to go on, she remembers that loving promise: I can do all things through Christ.

THE CONFIDENCE TO FOLLOW CHRIST UNCEASINGLY

Early Sunday morning,
while it was still dark,
Mary Magdalene came to the tomb
and found that the stone had been
rolled away from the entrance.

JOHN 20:1 NLT

Mary couldn't wait.

Her unwavering loyalty to Christ continued, even though He had died on the cross. She arose well before dawn and went to His grave to anoint His body with burial spices (see Mark 16:1), as one last task she could do for her Lord. Her discovery of the open tomb led to astonishment and grief, as she assumed the Romans had taken Him away. She ran to tell Peter and the "other disciple, whom Jesus loved," and they, too, saw that His body was gone, but they simply returned to their homes.

Mary waited.

Throughout the New Testament, while most of those around Jesus doubted, denied, or fled, Mary and some of the other women stayed by His side. They traveled with the disciples during good times, and they helped support Jesus' ministry financially (see Luke 8:1–3). Mary's devotion began the moment He freed her from seven demons, and she didn't abandon Him or her faith when His journey turned toward the crucifixion. She was not afraid of being associated with Jesus, and she followed him up Golgotha and down again to the tomb.

The reward for this devotion came as she waited by the empty tomb, weeping. Spotting a man she thought was the gardener, she begged for information about Jesus. Instead, she heard the voice she thought was gone forever. " 'Sir,' she said, 'if you have taken him away, tell me where you have put him, and I will go and get him.'

" 'Mary!' Jesus said.

"She turned toward him and exclaimed, 'Teacher!' " (John 20:15–16 NLT).

Mary Magdalene was the first person to see Jesus after His resurrection, the first to know that the prophecies were true, the first to discover that Christ was alive forever. Rejoicing, she ran to tell others of the good news.

Mary's loyalty reminds us that devoting our lives to the Lord isn't always simple. Allegiance to God takes determination as well as love. Many times, believers will lose the intensity they felt after their conversion, or they'll devote prayer time to Him only when they need something. Giving ourselves to Him, however, is the least we can do for the One who gave Himself so totally to us.

CONFIDENCE TO GO BEYOND

"Have I not commanded you?
Be strong and of good courage;
do not be afraid, nor be dismayed,
for the LORD your God is with you
wherever you go."

JOSHUA 1:9 NKJV

Sometimes confidence is found in the most unlikely of places. For writer, speaker, and interior designer Ann Platz, this place was the pantry of her new home.

Ann owns her own business, a successful design firm based in Atlanta, Georgia. Known for her elegant designs and sense of color, Ann's extensive list of satisfied clients continues to expand. The author of thirteen books, Ann speaks regularly to a variety of groups and has even written about the courage of women who have shown great faith in the face of adversity.

Past successes, however, don't always mean having confidence in future endeavors. Women who seek to grow and expand, in both their faith and their personal goals, often find themselves facing tasks that far exceed their current abilities. Or so they may believe.

Ann found an answer to those doubts when she moved into her new home. Ann writes, "I discovered this scripture, Joshua 1:9, printed on a business-sized card, in the pantry of my new home. The house had belonged to the estate of a woman I greatly admired, Mrs. Grace Kinser. Later I realized that this message 'left behind' would be a life message to me. I framed the card. Many a day I have been challenged beyond my abilities and have sought great spiritual strength and confidence from this printed message of grace from Grace."

What Ann discovered is the same courage available to any speaker with quaking legs, any businesswoman with doubts about her presentation, or any mother who worries whether she's making the right choices for her children. When we believe our own abilities will fail us, we can turn our minds and hearts outward, relying on the One who never fails. God, who is always with us, will give us the strength and courage to face—and conquer—whatever challenges lie before us.

THE CONFIDENCE TO LEAD

So [Apollos] began to speak boldly in the synagogue.
When Aquila and Priscilla heard him,
they took him aside and explained to him
the way of God more accurately.

ACTS 18:26 NKJV

Priscilla and her husband, Aquila, may have been the world's first husband-and-wife ministry team. They certainly set a standard for leadership, and Priscilla's equal partnership with Aquila stands as a reminder that God gives women ministerial gifts to use and reach others for Christ.

Priscilla and Aquila left Rome when the emperor Claudius expelled all the Jews. They settled in Corinth and established a tent-making business, working together. When Paul came to Corinth in AD 50, he stayed with them, working alongside them, since he, too, was a tentmaker by trade. This gave them an extraordinary opportunity to learn the gospel message, to question Paul, and to absorb the intricacies of Jesus' teachings. For the next eighteen months, the three of them worked to build the church in Corinth, and when Paul left, Priscilla and Aquila went with him as far as Ephesus.

These two were very influential in Ephesus, remaining after Paul left in order to teach and build a foundation for the believers there. They ran a house church (see 1 Corinthians 16:19), and in one of the most profound examples of their work, they watched the dynamic speaker

Apollos, recognizing his gifts but also the errors in his message. Instead of confronting him, however, they took him aside privately, offering him correction and encouragement (see Acts 18:26). Their goal was to strengthen the body of Christ, not humiliate someone making mistakes.

They remained staunch friends with Paul, however, who continued to greet them in his letters, even after they returned to Rome (see 2 Timothy 4:19).

Scholars have sometimes pointed to the fact that Priscilla is mentioned first as often as Aquila, which may indicate that Paul sees them as partners, equal in strength. Larry Richards, in his in-depth book *Every Woman in the Bible,* reflects on the creation of woman in Genesis and suggests, "In Priscilla and Aquila we see the transformation of marriage and the restoration of God's original intent that married couples should be partners in all things in their life."

Without a doubt, Priscilla and Aquila helped transform the early church, despite exile, threat of death (see Romans 16:4), or the need to make a living. Women can still look to Priscilla to see that women definitely should have the confidence to minister to others, when the need arises.

CONFIDENCE TO REACH
FOR THE STARS

*God. . .is able to accomplish infinitely more
than we would ever dare to ask or hope.*

EPHESIANS 3:20 NLT

Sometimes a simple verse from scripture can do much more than inspire confidence; sometimes it can change a life.

By the time she was sixteen, Allison Gappa Bottke's life was a chaotic shambles. A rebellious and confused teen, she had run away at the age of fifteen to marry a man who soon turned into her abuser, rapist, and attempted murderer. A year later, Allison was a mother, divorced, and firmly convinced that God didn't exist.

Allison struggled just to survive. Practical things, like school, work, and being a mother, filled her days, while her nights were filled with alcohol, drugs, and parties. Empty promises and even emptier pursuits filled her soul. She felt lost and worthless, as life became an unending series of unfulfilled dreams.

Then Allison took a walk that changed her life. Her stroll went past a neighborhood church, and she suddenly felt an overwhelming draw into the church. Alone in the balcony, she gazed toward the pulpit and saw a statue of Jesus with outstretched hands, looking right at her. Unfamiliar emotions filled her heart and soul, and there in the pew, Allison cried as she listened to the pastor talk about being lost, without direction, without hope, without faith—and how listening to the Holy Spirit and asking the Lord Jesus Christ to come into our hearts could change that. He would be there—just like that.

Allison wanted to know more about this relationship with Jesus. She studied, prayed, worshiped, and over the next ten years made a spiritual connection that turned her life around. She gave her life to Jesus, and where before she had felt only desolation, now her life was one of healing and hope.

Yet it was this simple verse in Ephesians that helped her turn her dreams over to Jesus, as well as her life.

The results stunned even her. She founded the God Allows U-Turns organization to show others how their lives can be changed, and the world opened up in ways she had never imagined. She asked God to fulfill His dreams for her, and He showered her and her family with blessings beyond comprehension.

Today, Allison continues to share the message that it is never too late to turn toward God, with both your heart and dreams. Doors really can fly open to make real Ephesians 3:20, the verse that has continued to give Allison confidence, that continues to inspire her to reach for the stars.

God, the Father, Always Supports You

I took Israel by the arm and taught them to walk.
But they would not admit that
I was the one who had healed them.
I led them with kindness and with love,
not with ropes. I held them close to me;
I bent down to feed them.

Hosea 11:3–4 CEV

With his red hair and bright blue eyes, Frank charmed most people just by learning to walk. I had known Frank since he was born, and I often dropped in to see him and his mom, Amy, especially when Frank reached that age where everything was an adventure, including this new skill called walking. He would grasp the edge of the coffee table with chubby little hands and pull himself up, then toddle to the end, still holding on to the table. Once his safety perch was gone, however, he'd hesitate, then take a step or two on wobbly legs.

Amy cheered him on from the wingback chair at the end of the room. Another step, and Frank would teeter and fall with a thump. Sometimes he'd just sit down. Other times he'd topple forward, catching himself with his hands. Immediately, Frank would look around.

"I'm here, baby," Amy said.

Satisfied, Frank crawled back to the table and started over, bouncing when he first pulled up with his own private glee.

"What happens when you're not here?" I asked.

Frank's mother leaned back against her

cushions. "He cries, and he stops trying. But as long as he knows I'm here, he keeps working at it." She grinned. "Kinda like us and God, huh?"

How true! No matter what God has called us to do, or how many skills we bring to the task, the journey is never completely smooth. Bumps and falls, large and small, fill the path. Scripture is filled with portrayals of God as a loving, nurturing parent, like this passage in Hosea, which reminds us that God's support continues throughout our lives—not just when we're in trouble. As Amy stood by, helping her son to walk and giving him the assurance he needed to continue, God always stands beside us, encouraging and comforting us, giving us the strength and confidence to continue on the way He has chosen for us.

THE COURAGE
TO INFLUENCE

One of them was Lydia,
who was from the city of Thyatira
and sold expensive purple cloth.
She was a worshiper of the Lord God,
and he made her willing to accept
what Paul was saying.
Then after she and her family were baptized,
she kept on begging us,
"If you think I really do have faith in the Lord,
come stay in my home."
Finally, we accepted her invitation.

ACTS 16:14–15 CEV

Lydia was a magnificent woman. Successful, intelligent, perceptive, and persuasive, she is the prime example of how Christian businesswomen have been influencing those around them since the first days of the church.

Originally from Thyatira, a city in the western province of Asia Minor, Lydia had moved to Philippi, where she made her living selling purple cloth, a luxurious fabric made from the shells of a mollusk. This cloth was rare, expensive, and usually bought only by the upper class. Because no husband or children are mentioned, and the household where she lived is referred to as hers, many scholars think she was single or widowed at a young age.

When Paul met Lydia, she was already a worshiper of God—even though she was a Gentile—and she had gathered at the river to worship Him with other like-minded women. When she heard Paul preach about Jesus and His redeeming work, the Lord "opened her heart," and she became Paul's first European convert and thus the first Christian businesswoman. Immediately, she wanted her entire household to be baptized and publicly insisted that Paul and Silas's team stay with her while they were in Philippi.

Embracing her newfound faith with the same energy and determination as she did her business, Lydia opened her home as a gathering place for other believers (see Acts 16:40). Apparently proud of her faith, Lydia was willing to do what she could to give Christians a home and a place to grow in Philippi.

Although Lydia is mentioned only twice in scripture, her enthusiasm for the Lord is contagious, and with Lydia as a role model, we should not hesitate to influence others toward Christ, and we don't have to be a wealthy entrepreneur to do it. No matter what our role in life, the confidence to share our faith comes from the power of the message of Jesus Christ.

GOD WILL COMPLETE HIS WORK IN YOU

Being confident of this very thing,
that he which hath begun a good work in you
will perform it until the day of Jesus Christ.

PHILIPPIANS 1:6 KJV

From a very early age, award-winning writer Cheryl Wolverton realized that God had a hand in her life. She was a "work in progress," and God would complete His "good work" in her. What she didn't know was that she was in for the ride of a lifetime.

Born into a loving family who raised her in the church, Cheryl met the love of her life, Steve, just as he was about to go into the army. Even though Cheryl had declared she'd never date a military man, Steve was irresistible. As Cheryl writes, "God knew what He was doing, even if I didn't. Steve is the calm to my craziness, the patience to my short temper."

Two beautiful children soon joined this well-balanced marriage, including a daughter who came six weeks early and a hyperactive son. Between her kids and the activity of a military marriage, however, Cheryl soon needed an escape and found it in her writing. She wrote several books, each time producing a novel built around what she thought the "world" wanted to read.

They didn't sell. Cheryl's explanation? They didn't have God in them, therefore, "they didn't contain 'me,'" she writes. They weren't within God's plan for her life. "I changed what I was writing, putting everything in me, including my faith, into these books." The first one sold in the fall of 1996. Since then, Cheryl has published twenty books, won numerous awards, and shared her story through her speaking engagements.

But God wasn't through with her just yet.

First came the diagnosis for some problems Cheryl had been having: multiple sclerosis. Still relying on God for support and strength, she refused to let MS drag her down. As she studied her disease, she learned how to manage her good days and her bad. In the midst of that battle, Cheryl felt led to go back and finish the college degree she'd stepped away from twenty years before to have her children.

Still, her escape continued to be her writing. Cheryl felt God leading her in yet another new direction. Setting aside her novels, Cheryl's work now focuses on nonfiction, specifically devotionals that she hopes will lead her readers closer to the heart of God.

This is a place she knows well. Since she was a child, Cheryl has found the confidence in God's Word to trust His direction, His "good work" for her journey.

CONFIDENCE TO
USE GOD'S GIFTS

Since you are so eager to have spiritual gifts,
ask God for those that will be
of real help to the whole church.

1 CORINTHIANS 14:12 NLT

I am amazed at how often my own words come back to haunt me. Of course, as much as I talk, I shouldn't be surprised. In this case, it happened because I asked my pastor what I could do for the church. I've often been told that our talents are a gift from God; what we do with them is our gift to Him. Taking confidence from this verse from Paul, I thought I might be useful as a teacher or office volunteer. Although I didn't specify what I wanted to do, my pastor assured me that he was sure there would be a way for me to serve the church.

Two days later, he called. "The nominating committee wants you to chair the pastor-parish relations committee," he said, sounding tremendously confident.

I, on the other hand, had trouble breathing. "Jim, I don't have enough experience to do that. I've only been on the committee one year. We met three times, and I missed one of those!"

"Don't worry. You only have to meet when there are staff changes or when it's time to decide whether or not you want a new pastor."

I was still doubtful, so God and I sat down to have a little talk. (Actually, I did most of the talking.) "But there are a lot of other folks who have more knowledge than I do." My protests were beginning to sound a little like Moses, and I said so to God. Like Moses, I knew I had to do this—and like Moses, I knew God would be with me.

I just hoped He wouldn't require me to head toward water. I'm a lousy swimmer.

My call to agree delighted Jim. "Don't worry. It'll be easy. Our staff is stable. There won't be any changes this year." I got no consolation out of the fact that Jim publicly repented of those words six months later.

Within weeks of my saying yes, our pianist, the secretary, a nursery worker, and the choir director all resigned. And, of course, there was that surprise phone call from the chair of the finance committee about my budget.

"Budget?" I asked, thinking about the Jackson Pollock artwork that passed for my checkbook. "What budget?"

I did a lot of talking to God that year, but I made it through. Good thing—after all, you never know what God might have up His sleeve. For instance, I have recently had this desire to be close to water.

THE CONFIDENCE
TO SERVE

In Joppa there was a follower named Tabitha.
Her Greek name was Dorcas, which means "deer."
She was always doing good things for people
and had given much to the poor.

ACTS 9:36 CEV

From the time that Jesus began His ministry through the travels of His disciples, scripture is filled with people who came to them, asking for healing. Dorcas, on the other hand, never seemed to ask for anything, either from Peter or her friends. Instead, her heart was set on serving, and one of her greatest gifts was the love she had for others.

Dorcas lived in Joppa, a beautiful seacoast town about thirty-five miles from Jerusalem. Beautiful, but sometimes harsh, since many of the men made a living on the sea. Losing a husband or son was a frequent occurrence for the women there. Dorcas saw this and responded to the need. Although she was a widow herself, Dorcas didn't dwell in or on the past. She kept moving forward with her life, "doing good things," and providing other widows and those in need with clothes she had sewn herself. Some Bible translations call her a "disciple," which is the only time that this title is used for a woman. She may have served the local church as a deaconess.

No wonder, then, that when she suddenly fell ill and died, the believers in Joppa who adored her so much immediately sent for Peter. When he arrived, they were mourning her, but the widows grabbed him, showing Peter all the garments she'd made for them. Peter was moved by their devotion, and he sent them away. Kneeling by her bed to pray, Peter called her name and said simply, "Arise."

She did, and Peter took her out and presented her to the other widows. Before long, everyone in the area knew about her healing, which resulted in many of them coming to the Lord.

All because Dorcas had the heart and confidence to serve others.

Being a servant is not easy. The work is hard and long. But when that work is done in the name of the Lord, even the simplest skill with a needle and thread can become a great tool for evangelism. Servanthood is a gift, and Dorcas clearly demonstrated that when we have the confidence to serve in small ways, great things can be the result.

GOD HAS ALWAYS BEEN THERE

For You are my hope, O Lord GOD;
You are my trust from my youth.
By You I have been upheld from birth;
You are He who took me out of
my mother's womb. My praise
shall be continually of You.

PSALM 71:5–6 NKJV

Gail began having little prayer sessions with God when she was only twelve. Inspired by a devout Sunday school teacher, Gail believed that these little talks with the Lord would cement a relationship with Him in her heart. "I would walk around my yard, huddled in this raggedy old coat, just talking out loud to God, like He was there next to me. Little did I know," she said later, "how much that would mean through the years."

In her late teens, Gail left the church, turning to a variety of New Age beliefs. "I've stood on the mountain and helped my coven raise the 'cone of power.' I've burned sage to cleanse my house, and put out black salt. Crystals decorated my living room. I've done workshops on 'finding the goddess within.'" Yet these beliefs did little for Gail's heart and mind when life's inevitable trials raged through her life. "In less than a month, my marriage collapsed and two of my friends were murdered. My world rocked, and I found myself thinking less about tarot card readings and crystals, and more about God's love for me. And I realized that no matter what path I had taken, He'd always been there."

Gail turned back to scripture, finding Psalm 71. "That was the message I'd been missing," she told me over coffee one day. "I was the one who'd moved away, but He had never abandoned me. It was God's unceasing presence in my life that gave me the confidence to work through what was happening. And only God."

Gail picked up where she left off, wandering around her yard, talking out loud to God. "My coat is nicer and my friends don't think I'm as weird, but embracing God's eternal presence changed my life. He didn't leave me; I'm not leaving Him again."

YOU WILL CONQUER

*Yet in all these things we are more than
conquerors through Him who loved us.*

ROMANS 8:37 NKJV

I just don't understand," Kate said, her fists clenched in anger, "how he could stand up before our church—our pastor—and lie!"

This was the opening volley in an evening-long conversation with a woman in a lot of pain. Kate's faith—and her marriage—were only a few months old, and both were collapsing around her. The deception and betrayal of her young husband wrenched her heart, but that he had professed a faith that he had not truly held threatened to shred her newfound love of God.

After several hours, we wound up talking about Romans 8, with Paul's depiction of a world corrupted by sin and redeemed by God. We discussed that while this "bad news/good news" message had a global scale, it also applied to much of our own lives. The word "tribulation" that Paul uses in verse 35 works on two levels, meaning emotional stress as well as troubles caused by external factors. Kate slowly calmed down as we talked about those friends who had dealt with devastating illness, emerging stronger and wiser. From the ashes of a fire-stricken home had come a family with a renewed bond and determination to survive. In her own case, an abusive relationship had put Kate on the path that eventually had led her to find the Lord.

Most of all, we talked about God's love.

When God sent His Son to save His children, He definitely worked a grand plan for the universe. But He also had each one of us in mind, as well. No matter what trials we experience in this life, He never stops loving us. He died for us—He's certainly not about to abandon us when we need Him most. He loves us and wants us to conquer, to succeed, no matter what the world throws at us.

CONFIDENCE TO PASS
ON YOUR FAITH

I have been reminded of your sincere faith,
which first lived in your grandmother Lois
and in your mother Eunice and,
I am persuaded, now lives in you also.

2 TIMOTHY 1:5 NIV

It's a truism we hear repeated all the time: Parents are the single greatest influence on their children. Children watch and listen, especially when they're young, absorbing the way their parents act as well as listening to what they say. This is one reason that Lois and Eunice have been recognized for passing on their "genuine faith," taking care to teach Timothy the holy scriptures, an important step in leading him to be "wise for salvation through faith" (2 Timothy 3:15 NIV).

Lois and Eunice were Jews, who had most likely been converted by Paul when he stopped in Lystra during his first missionary journey. Already grounded with a firm faith in the Lord, they accepted Christ and continued to grow and practice their new faith with an unwavering confidence. Timothy, because of the sound background his mother and grandmother had given him, also accepted the call to Jesus, becoming a second-generation leader in the new church.

Handing down our faith across the generations is a vital gift we can give our children, and the bonds across the years don't have to be blood alone. Many of the wisest people in our lives may be our spiritual kin and unrelated by genetics. Each generation has great gifts to share in wisdom, life experiences, and a deeper understanding of scripture that sometimes comes just through walking with Christ for decades.

Mothers to daughters, grandmothers to granddaughters, mentors to the younger people in their spiritual care. We all can look at the beautiful lessons that Lois and Eunice passed on, and we can see the need and have the confidence to reach out to our own. Although we have no idea what kind of adults they will become, the teachings of the Lord will remain with them forever.

The Confidence to Obey God, Not Man

Then Peter and the other apostles answered and said,
We ought to obey God rather than men.

Acts 5:29 kjv

Phoebe Palmer's ministry was literally forged in the flames.

Born in 1807, Phoebe had been raised Methodist, although her own spirituality had not been emotional or spectacular in any way. She grew up, married a doctor, and had three children. After her first two children died, she focused her energy on little Eliza, who was barely eleven months old on July 29, 1836, when Phoebe put her to bed for the last time. A few hours later, a servant tried to fill the oil lamp in Eliza's nursery without extinguishing the flame first, and the fire swept over Eliza's crib. Although they put out the blaze quickly, Eliza died a few hours later.

Grief consumed Phoebe, and she spent long hours in prayer, finally realizing that she was being called to use the time she had showered on her children to teach others about Christ. She attended meetings held by her sister that focused on a "holiness" theology and by 1840 was leading them, developing her own revolutionary stance, which was a simpler form of Wesley's doctrine of perfection. Phoebe's "altar theology" was based on a threefold approach: consecration, faith, and testimony.

Believers were called to dedicate themselves and their lives to the Lord, followed by a strongly professed belief in Jesus Christ. They were then called on to tell the world about their faith.

Simple, but Phoebe's call to holiness carried her across the globe. She ignored critics of her theology, her looks, and her feminist views, and spoke at hundreds of camp meetings, sparking a revival movement that brought more than one hundred thousand believers to God. She preached overseas, bringing the same revivalism to the United Kingdom.

Returning to the States, Phoebe shifted her work toward the urban poor, putting her faith into direct action. She still spoke at meetings, but now she worked in the streets, doing what she could to improve the conditions in the slums. Her husband provided free medical care, and Phoebe opened a mission house in Five Points, the worst slum in New York City. When she couldn't get out of the city, she wrote, finishing eighteen books and editing a magazine, *Guide to Holiness*, for eleven years.

Phoebe never cared much for the dictates of her social class, preferring God's approval to that of her fellow man. As a result, she forever changed holiness theology and the spirit of reform in the inner cities. When she died in 1874, condolences poured in from around the world, praising the work of one woman who was confident to follow the path God had prescribed for her, no matter what anyone else said.

CONFIDENCE FROM A PARENT'S LOVE

*"I will be a Father to you,
and you shall be My sons and daughters,
says the LORD Almighty."*

2 CORINTHIANS 6:18 NKJV

Do you think it's silly," Stephanie asked softly, "to pray about Madeline's soft-ball game?"

Stephanie, my hairstylist, gives me a color and cut once a month. Madeline is her daughter, and we often talk about the usual stylist/client topics like kids, school, and work. Since she found out I'm a Christian writer, however, she also asks questions about faith that sometimes send me scurrying back to the scriptures for answers. Over the past few years, we've discussed divorce and infidelity, abortion, political involve-ment, and taxes.

This, however, wasn't one of those questions. "Why would you think it's silly?"

"This guy told me I shouldn't pray about trivial stuff like that. I mean, I'm not praying for her team to win or anything, although I hope they do. I just pray she has a good game and learns something. Softball has been really good for her."

"So why do you think that's trivial?"

She snipped a strand of hair. "I don't. He did. I was wondering what you thought."

I looked at her in the mirror. "Don't you find that whatever is important to Madeline is important to you, if only because you're her mom and you love her?"

She grinned. "Like God the Father."

"We're His children. Would Madeline be playing softball if you didn't love and support her?"

"Probably not. She can be determined, but I don't think she'd keep going if I didn't back her up. Or drive her to the games." Stephanie fluffed my wet hair, then combed through it again, pulling strands on each side to make sure she'd trimmed them evenly. "So you think that we should have confidence to do what we set out to do, because God loves us like a Father."

"That's what scripture tells us."

"Even when we pray for our kids' softball games?"

"Especially when we pray for our kids."

GOD CHOOSES YOU

Coming to Him as to a living stone,
rejected indeed by men, but chosen by God
and precious, you also, as living stones,
are being built up a spiritual house,
a holy priesthood, to offer up spiritual sacrifices
acceptable to God through Jesus Christ.

1 PETER 2:4–5 NKJV

Born only two years before the first women's rights convention in 1850, Mary Slessor gave the world a whole new meaning to the idea of freedom for women.

Redheaded and bright-eyed, Mary knew even as a child that she wanted to be a missionary. She felt God had chosen her to follow in David Livingstone's footsteps, even though she had some growing up to do first. When her family moved to Dundee in 1859, she took a job in a jute mill, working half a day, then going to school the other half. By the age of fourteen, she was a skilled weaver who diligently continued her studies.

At twenty-eight, she finally realized her dream and was assigned to Calabar by the Foreign Mission Board. There she created quite a stir by going against all the norms for women missionaries. Abandoning her corsets and veils, she dressed in the style of the tribes she worked with and learned to speak Efik, so that she could use humor and sarcasm in her confrontations with some tribal customs.

And confront she did! She had a great respect for the people among whom she lived, and they understood that. This respect gave her freedom to attack such practices as ritual killing of twins, who were thought to be conceived by devils. Mary convinced the tribal leaders that twins were a sign of male virility instead. She also worked for more dignity for women and battled the enslavement of girls and wives. One anecdote told of Mary Slessor was that she once came upon a group of men assaulting a young woman and attacked them so fiercely with her umbrella that they fled.

Mary's confidence to do God's will knew no bounds, and the local tribes in West Africa embraced her, calling her the "mother of all peoples." She continued to work deeper into the heart of the country, loving the people and bringing them messages of hope and freedom as well as the Word of God. She lived longer than many of her missionary colleagues, which some thought due to her sheer will to survive. She succumbed to a fever in January 1915 at the age of sixty-six.

Mary Slessor, with her love of God and her determination to help people, stands as a model to prove exactly how much can be done when we have confidence in the God-chosen path for our lives.

God Renews You

He gives power to the weak, and to those
who have no might He increases strength.
Even the youths shall faint and be weary,
and the young men shall utterly fall,
but those who wait on the LORD shall renew
their strength; they shall mount up with
wings like eagles, they shall run and not be weary,
They shall walk and not faint.

Isaiah 40:29–31 NKJV

It had been one of those weeks. I was going to move the next weekend, and no matter how closely I attended to the details, I had convinced myself that my moving day was going to be a disaster. No one would show up to help me; all my plans would go awry. By Friday, my mind and body were drained, and I had yet to lift a single box.

Finally, I called a dear friend. It was time for prayer, and a lot of it.

When I was younger, I thought I had coped with most tough days and rough trials through the strength of my own reasoning skills and intelligence. When I couldn't handle it on my own, I counted on my own strength and the strength of friends' and family's help and support. This could be the physical strength needed to move a large sofa or the psychological support to weather a difficult life situation or make a life-changing decision.

As time marched on, however, I found that the strengths I thought were unsurpassed seemed to vary and fade and fluctuate. They really hadn't; I just had more life experiences and time was the teacher. I was confronted time and again with the fact that by myself, I was limited. I was even limited when my friends and family did their best to assist me in whatever endeavor I pursued. No matter how loyal friends are, they aren't always available when you really need them.

Finally, during a particularly dark period in my life, after twisting and turning to "make it happen"—and after I'd beaten my head against enough walls—I collapsed, completely exhausted in mind, body, and spirit. My pride broke as I found all avenues blocked, and I felt whipped and beaten down.

The clay was ready for the Potter. I gave my situation and myself totally over to the Lord.

That's when God stepped in.

As the doors opened to a solution, I saw all too clearly that He was the One from whom all strength and power came. That in the honest and true admission of my weaknesses, and by coming to God, real, lasting, unshakable strength could be found.

When you recognize your need for a God-centered life, you will be uplifted and carried by His love and strength daily, renewed and buoyed by the confidence that springs from drawing His power.

GOD TURNS WEAKNESSES INTO STRENGTHS

And he said unto me, My grace is sufficient for thee: for my strength is made perfect in weakness. Most gladly therefore will I rather glory in my infirmities, that the power of Christ may rest upon me. Therefore I take pleasure in infirmities, in reproaches, in necessities, in persecutions, in distresses for Christ's sake: for when I am weak, then am I strong.

2 CORINTHIANS 12:9–10 KJV

Fanny Crosby would no doubt agree with Paul's words about his infirmities. Blinded when she was six weeks old by a man posing as a doctor, she never wasted a moment in anger or self-pity, later writing, "I have not for a moment in more than eighty-five years felt a spark of resentment against him, because I have always believed that the good Lord by this means consecrated me to the work that I am still permitted to do."

A gifted, prolific poet, Fanny was already well-known for her readings and published poetry by the time she was accepted at the Institute for the Blind when she was fifteen. With a mind like quicksilver, she memorized great works of literature, including most of the Bible. She remained a student at the institute for twelve years, then was a teacher there for eleven. All the while her poetry circled the globe, and the young girl found that by eighteen she was receiving visits from presidents and dignitaries. At twenty-three she stood before the U.S. Congress, and at twenty-four published her first book.

But she was not yet a Christian.

Fanny had loved the language of the Bible, but its message had never opened her heart.

Finally, at thirty-one, she received the Lord in a revival meeting, describing her own conversion as a flash of "celestial light." God touched her mind and soul, and the floodgates opened.

Over the next sixty years, Fanny wrote more than eighty-five hundred hymns, sometimes as many as seven a day! Inspiration came to her from everywhere, from ordinary sources, such as a carriage ride, to events that rocked her life, like the death of her infant daughter, for whom she wrote "Safe in the Arms of Jesus."

What Fanny could not see, she could feel, and God's love and blessings on her set aside her blindness in favor of a wisdom and a "sight" that few other people have experienced. Yet all of us can follow her example in finding the confidence to use what gifts God has bestowed on us, no matter what "infirmities" challenge our everyday lives.

GOD HELPS YOU OVERCOME

And I will bring the blind by a way they knew not;
I will lead them in paths they have not known:
I will make darkness light before them, and crooked
things straight. These things I will do unto them,
and not forsake them.

ISAIAH 42:16 KJV

What has been your experience with blindness? Perhaps you've known someone who is sight impaired or completely blind and have talked about these challenges intimately. Or maybe you've been in a blackout. What can be scarier than suddenly being in one of today's modern buildings, with its maze of windowless cubicles, or in a transit system that leaves you a thousand feet underground in pitch-blackness? So there you are, trying to decide whether to sit tight or take your chances trying to find your way to a lighted area, even though the path may be crooked and full of obstacles.

Maybe you played blindman's bluff as a child, with your eyes scrunched shut, cautiously edging about trying to grab someone so they could be "it." Perhaps you were wearing a kerchief over your eyes, wildly trying to strike a piñata.

Isaiah, however, is not referring to a blindness made by a game, or physical disease, or the lack of light from a lamp. In this song of praise (Isaiah 42:10–17), he's talking about a blindness that comes from inside a heart and soul that has been spiritually lazy, a blindness from which many people suffer, a self-inflicted blindness created by selfishness, ignorance, and self-serving purposes.

This blindness is one that separates us from all the spiritual beauty, strength, and confidence that God offers us through our acceptance of Him as our Lord. Yet Isaiah also wants us to know that if we will trust God and His designs for our lives, we never need to fear any darkness again; we never need to fear being misled or lost. When we give ourselves over to God, regardless of whether the paths we travel are familiar or strange, we can be assured that we are safe, led by Someone who will not forsake us or leave us in the dark if things get rough.

God walks with us, and when we are too weak to walk He carries us. In His wisdom, He will help us overcome our obstacles, our "blindness," to become who He knows we can be. And with God lighting our way, we can feel confident that nothing is impossible to overcome.

TRUST IN THE LORD BUILDS CONFIDENCE

This is what the LORD says:
"Cursed are those who put their trust
in mere humans and turn their
hearts away from the LORD.
They are like stunted shrubs in the desert,
with no hope for the future.
They will live in the barren wilderness,
on the salty flats where no one lives.
But blessed are those who trust in the LORD
and have made the LORD their hope and confidence."

JEREMIAH 17:5–7 NLT

Amma?" The small girl's dark eyes brightened with tears as she used the Tamil word for mother. Amy Carmichael looked down at the Indian child who had been brought to her by a woman Amy had recently converted. "Amma," the girl repeated, "I want to stay with you."

It wasn't the first time Amy's heart had melted since arriving in Dohnavur, India, in 1895, when she was only twenty-eight years old. Sent by the Church of England's Zenana Missionary Society, Amy hadn't been quite sure what she was going to do there. Yet she had dedicated herself to the Lord and to missionary service, and she trusted Him to lead her. She had no idea that she was about to spend the next fifty-six years in Dohnavur, never even taking a furlough to return home to her family.

Preena, the child who called her Amma, became one of the hundreds of reasons why. At seven, Preena had already been sold to a local temple to be trained as a prostitute. She would work in the temple for a few years, but would begin servicing the local men of the temple by the time she was ten or eleven.

Amy had found her mission for God. She

began striving furiously to improve the status of women in the culture, and she fought to save as many of the child prostitutes as she could. This work led to the founding of the Dohnavur Fellowship, which raised money and opened group homes for the girls first, then one for the boys, as well as a community hospital. In between her duties with the homes and hospital, Amy wrote about her experiences as well as her faith. The thirty-five books she produced are poignant testimonies to the trust she placed in her Lord as well as the blessings He bestowed upon her.

Amy didn't choose to go to India; she was sent. Her trust in the Lord, however, gave her the confidence to go willingly wherever He needed her, and the world has cherished the result ever since.

GOD PROTECTS YOU

I will lift up mine eyes unto the hills,
from whence cometh my help.
My help cometh from the LORD,
which made heaven and earth.

PSALM 121:1–2 KJV

Donna seemed to have it all. An undeniable physical beauty was matched with a sweet, gentle spirit. She loved her Lord and her husband. Yet when I first met her, Donna was struggling with a consuming fear of open places and people. Agoraphobia had robbed her of much of her joy, and no level of counseling had so far broken through the cause or found a solution.

No matter how pleasant our lives can be, in every life fears, dangers, and anxieties can work their way in to our spirit. Some are founded on tangible facts. Some are situations we have created through bad choices. Others can be lurking in each person's mind, like Donna's, the thoughts that come unbidden in the middle of the night, or perhaps while driving the kids to school or washing the dishes.

All fear, real or imagined, can damage our spirits as it tries to separate us from God and our true selves. How can we make clear choices in our lives when we allow our fears to rule us? We can't. But even more troublesome is that fear can cloud our view of the depth of God's love for each of us.

How can we refuse to let this fear or danger overwhelm us? I do it by simply remembering the grace and unconditional love that God extends to each of us, that, just as any father would, He protects and guides His children. And if we are fearful or in a difficult situation, we only need to ask for His help and intervention: "I will lift up mine eyes unto the hills, from whence cometh my help."

Donna's help came from an unexpected source: the children of her church. A young mother who had visited Donna saw how much her troubled friend enjoyed playing with her new baby. Slowly, she started showing up with more and more children from the church at Donna's house. They would romp and play, and familiarity with them eventually gave Donna the confidence to return to the church. She still sat at the back next to the door, and she still couldn't return to her job, but each small inroad held great promise.

God, our Father, will hear our cries and distress, and by and in our faith He will provide for our physical and emotional needs.

GOD RESCUES

And call upon me in the day of trouble:
I will deliver thee, and thou shalt glorify me.

PSALM 50:15 KJV

Ann Judson's short, adventurous life was not the one she'd dreamed of as a small child in Bradford, Massachusetts, where she was born in 1789. Although she read the Bible and prayed as a young girl, she didn't fully give her life over to Christ until 1806, when a religious revival swept through New England. Drawn more and more to the idea of missionary service as she finished her education, Ann continued to hold to that dream, even as she took a teaching position.

Three years later, when she was twenty-one, Ann met Adoniram Judson, a young minister, at a missions meeting hosted by her father. They married in 1812 and immediately set sail for the Far East, becoming the first American missionaries in Burma. The young couple adapted quickly to the local culture and dress, and the Burmese welcomed them, even if converts were few. In fact, the Judsons spent more than five years winning over the first ten, but those ten became the basis for almost all the missionary activity in the area for years to come.

Spreading the Word of God was not Ann's only mission, however. She used her teaching skills to reach out to the Burmese women, most of whom weren't allowed any education at all. Adoniram used his other skills as well, translating most of the New Testament into the local language.

Their conversion efforts were interrupted, however, when Burma and Britain went to war. Accused of being a British spy, Adoniram was imprisoned for more than eighteen months. Ann went to work providing food and clothing for her husband and some of the other prisoners, often having to smuggle it in. Disease ran rampant through the dungeon-like prison, and Ann's provisions kept many of the prisoners, including her husband, alive. When Adoniram was transferred, Ann packed up her children and belongings and followed him, beginning her supply system all over again.

The efforts took their toll, however, and in 1826, Ann contracted spotted fever. She died a short time after Adoniram was finally released from prison.

Despite the hardships, Ann simply never gave up. When asked how she had the courage and the determination to push on, she replied that she had done as God instructed in Psalm 50: "And call upon me in the day of trouble: I will deliver thee, and thou shalt glorify me."

GOD HAS CONFIDENCE IN YOU

He delivered me from my strong enemy,
and from them which hated me:
for they were to strong for me.
They prevented me in the day of my calamity:
but the LORD was my stay.
He brought me forth also into a large place;
he delivered me, because he delighted in me.

PSALM 18:17–19 KJV

How many times have your prayers been answered? How many times has God taken care of you? Your friends and family? What stressful situations have you passed through, trusting God to guide and protect you? How many times has it "worked out," when others thought it would not?

Perhaps you can think of an occasion that you trusted God to move actively in your life, the saving of a dear friend from disease, or perhaps a loved one's safe return home during a time of war, despite a life-threatening injury. Maybe it was during a difficult period in your youth, when confusion about where you "fit in" led to some ill-made choices for your life.

At some point in our lives, our obstacles, our "calamities," may prevent us from living a godly life, from following the true path God has ordained for us. And, yes, we may find it terrifying to acknowledge that we are over-whelmed. Yet, if we trust in the Lord and give our lives over to Him, we can clearly see that "He brought me forth also into a large place; he delivered me, because he delighted in me" (Psalm 18:19).

Think about that! He delights in us! By believing in God's grace and love, by trusting

Him in the face of any and all situations, we find confidence to deal with our troubles out of the infinite hope, strength, and ultimately wisdom that comes from loving the Lord. Nothing pleases God more than this, and by so doing we have acknowledged and allowed God's will and words into our hearts and minds.

God knows your potential; He never gives up on you. He has confidence in the person you are right now and the person you can become.

GOD IS THE SOURCE OF YOUR STRENGTH

My health may fail, and my spirit may grow weak,
but God remains the strength of my heart;
he is mine forever.

PSALM 73:26 NLT

Susanna Wesley is the perfect example of how influential a mother can be on not only her children but the world at large. Anyone intimidated by the "good wife" of Proverbs 31 should take a second look at Susanna, whose life can make most of us weak in the knees.

Born in 1669, Susanna was one of twenty-five children born to Samuel Annesley, a minister who filled his house with a broad range of people, some of them famous men of politics and academia. The lively—and crowded—household was filled with debate and dissent, and curious Susanna took it all in, learning Greek, Hebrew, theology, and literature from her father and his friends.

In 1688 she married Samuel Wesley, a young Church of England minister. The marriage was fruitful, if not particularly happy. The first nineteen years of her marriage Susanna gave birth to nineteen children, although nine of them died while still infants. Her home burned twice, once almost taking five-year-old John with it. Her grief, multiple births, and poor living conditions left the young woman ill much of the time, but Susanna didn't give up or dwell on her hardships. With money tight and her husband often gone, Susanna grew even more determined to give her children the kind of education and home life she had growing up.

So began her Sunday evening meetings. In addition to the standard lessons she gave the children, these discussions centered around scripture reading and the sermons they had heard that morning. They were intended just for family, but word soon spread, and before long a crowd started showing up. At a time when most women weren't allowed to speak in church, much less the pulpit, Susanna Wesley found the strength and confidence to speak to more than two hundred people every week.

The profound impact her determination had on her children cannot be denied. Charles wrote more than eighteen hundred hymns, and her son John went on to change the face of Christianity. While Susanna's health was frequently weak, her strength and confidence came from the One who never fails.

GOD IS THERE WHEN YOU FAIL

If you do what the LORD wants,
he will make certain each step you take is sure.
The LORD will hold your hand, and if you stumble,
you still won't fall.

PSALM 37:23–24 CEV

Barb knew the goal she'd set out for herself—starting her own business—was a daunting one, but she was careful. She began with the best intentions and laid out her plans for success. She budgeted carefully and consulted with some successful businesswomen in her same field. She tried to do all tasks in a godly manner, keeping to the high road, trying to follow God's teachings, remembering to ask actively and to be guided by His Word and will in her daily life and in her decisions. She put her trust in the Lord to see her through, and she did her very best to succeed.

Only she didn't.

"I kept hearing the same litany over and over in my head," she told me, when I was thinking of starting my own business. "I'd failed. I'd become a loser. I'd fallen short." She grimaced. "But even worse, you know what was the first thing I did? Did I ask God for more help and guidance, for redirection? Oh, no. No, the first thing I did was to check who'd seen me do this. How many people knew the magnitude of my failure? And inevitably how many people could I prevent from finding out my shame in failure?"

She opened her Bible and showed me this

passage from Psalm 37. "You see, I had this idea that just because I believed, I'd succeed. When I didn't, it was a huge blow, like I'd let everyone down, including God. But when I slowed down to think about it, I knew I'd done my best. I knew in my heart I'd tried to do everything in a godly manner. So where was my shame? There was none. What was there to hide? There was nothing to conceal. Why care who knew? The Lord is who I wish to please and serve, not man.

"I was having all these negative thoughts because I'd forgotten God's infinite grace and love for me, I'd forgotten the 'The Lord will hold your hand,' and that even though I'd fallen short with my business, God was still right there with me. I'd stumbled, but because of His grace, I hadn't fallen."

Barb felt confident that because the Lord knew her heart and mind, He knew she'd tried her best. Knowing that God was still there, holding her hand and looking into her heart, gave her the confidence to try again.

GOD HEARS YOUR CRY FOR HELP

I waited patiently for the LORD;
and he inclined unto me, and heard my cry.
He brought me up also out of
an horrible pit, out of the miry clay,
and set my feet upon a rock,
and established my goings.
And he hath put a new song in my mouth,
even praise unto our God:
many shall see it, and fear,
and shall trust in the LORD.

PSALM 40:1–3 KJV

Marcheta, whom I've known for many years, is a beautiful portrait of how God can change a life. A child of the sixties and seventies, the clichéd catchphrase of the time—"sex, drugs, and rock 'n' roll"—was a guiding force in her life. As she writes, "I can remember a time in my life when every choice I made was wrong, motivated by greed instead of good intentions or godly values. It was an I-me-mine-centered universe of fun and good times, without cares, commitments, or responsibilities to be accepted. I was chasing after the world, despite having been raised as a Christian."

As she got older, Marcheta began to see the consequences of her actions in her own life, as well as in the lives of people she loved. A lifestyle that had once been "fun" was now a frightening pit, full of desperation.

Her own words tell how she discovered that she needed to be pulled "out of the miry clay."

"This was a hole I had created for myself. More than anything, I needed to set my feet on 'that rock who is the Lord,' to repent and not deceive myself any longer, to allow Him to refresh my spirit and release me from my own bonds, the bonds I'd forged and maintained for years."

Marcheta started by praying for His forgiveness and asking for help in turning her life around. "I repented. I tried to sin no more, or lead others astray by my words or deeds. And regardless of how unworthy I felt, regardless of my past, I knew the Lord would hear my prayers, and He could change my heart and my mind and renew my spirit and life."

And did God ever hear her cry. Marcheta is now a living witness to God's love and life-changing power for all to see. Her new spirit has amazed many of her old friends, and the impact she's made on them is immeasurable. She is a walking example of why we should have confidence in God's ability to forgive, uplift, and move us on in our lives.

CONFIDENCE TO ACT

Dear brothers and sisters,
what's the use of saying you have faith
if you don't prove it by your actions?
That kind of faith can't save anyone.

JAMES 2:14 NLT

Sometimes God plants you where He wants you, whether you want to go there or not. In my case, it was a call about a job that came out of the blue. I hadn't applied for it; didn't even know that such a job as "Bible Editor" even existed. I had recently hit another one of the many "rock bottoms" I've hit in my life, and I needed help. Once again, I'd asked for help, for God to open all the right doors.

Two weeks later, I was a Bible editor, overseeing the development of the study notes and annotations for a new study Bible. I can be kind of slow sometimes, though, especially where God is concerned, and I had been in the job a few weeks before I realized that I hadn't gotten the job because I needed the money. God had put me in this job because I needed a spiritual kick in the pants.

My faith was all over the place. While I believed in Jesus Christ as my Savior, that belief was an intellectual one; it had not really imbedded itself in my heart. While I had studied Greek in college and translated part of the New Testament, my understanding of scripture was from an academic point of view. Working with the Bible text day in and day out, eight hours a day, however, changed my life. The Bible came alive to me as a unit, a single salvation story, in a way it never had before. My heart opened, and I started asking more questions of God, of my supervisor, of myself.

This verse in James really made me sit up straighter and take a closer look of what I did believe. Had I changed? Did I act in ways that reflected my beliefs?

The answer, at that time, was "yes" and "no." Some of my actions continued to show my old way of thinking about life. But I was changing, and James's words helped me understand that this was a change that God wanted, and they gave me the confidence to look for new ways to share a growing faith and a life-changing belief in God's saving power.

And I've learned that when God wants you in His service, He wants all of you.

CONFIDENCE FROM RESPECT FOR GOD

Is not your reverence your confidence?
And the integrity of your ways your hope?

JOB 4:6 NKJV

Some of the worst advice I've ever had has come from well-meaning friends. Whether the advice was about work, men, or a trip I wanted to take, some of it was pretty lousy. Early last year, for instance, I was offered a project that I wanted to do, but I didn't think I had the time or the energy. My gut feeling told me to turn it down. All of my friends, however, thought it would be a great challenge for me, something I could sink my teeth into. Still. . .I knew that, for some reason, I was being led away from it.

It wound up being the hardest project I'd ever tackled. It gave me the most problems, and although I made the deadline, I spent quite a few sleepless nights getting there. It wasn't my best work, but the challenges of the work sent me back to my knees a lot, so it renewed my prayer life and my reverence for God. I do need to trust my instincts, however, since that's often the very place God works the hardest on us.

Job knew this to the bottom of his broken heart. He knew very well that he had not sinned or turned his back on God. While much of the advice he receives from his three friends in this section of the book of Job goes wildly astray, some of it is sound.

One of the more astute questions that Eliphaz asks, for instance, is this one regarding Job's reverence for God and his personal integrity. Obviously the answer is, in part, yes. There is confidence to be found in a deep, abiding reverence for the Lord, and a high standard of integrity provides a level of hope when life shakes our foundation.

Eliphaz, however, was using a basically sound principle to ridicule his friend and to suggest that Job's previous outburst was embarrassing and irreverent. Which isn't true, either. God loves us, and He understands our most intimate emotions. He understands anger and frustration, and even a touch of self-pity when things are beating us down. His shoulders are certainly big enough to withstand a few screams in His direction.

The difference is being able to get up, deal with the emotions, and find a new path. This isn't always something that can be done quickly or easily. We may need help from professionals or our friends (although not friends like Job's!). God knows we may need time to recover and heal.

Having a reverence for God, however, and a personal relationship with His Son can make all the difference in the world in having the confidence to pick up the pieces and rebuild.

Confidence in God's Wisdom

Trust in the LORD with all your heart,
and lean not on your own understanding;
in all your ways acknowledge Him and
He shall direct your paths.

Proverbs 3:5–6 NKJV

I looked at the e-mail again, thinking I'd misread it. Nope. It still said, simply, "That job is still open."

I almost couldn't believe it, and I turned my eyes toward heaven, whispering, "Thanks."

It was the open door I'd prayed for the night before, when I'd gone to my knees in desperation. Weeks of depression and struggles over work had culminated with yet another surrender to God and a plea for help. "I can't do this anymore, Lord. I'm tired of fighting, unsure if I'm going in the right direction. It's all Yours."

It wasn't the first time God had heard this from me—nor the first time I had confidence that He would provide. Over the past twenty years, "rock bottom" has become familiar territory to me. My cycles of depression were often triggered by my struggles to deal with my daughter's disabilities and her recurring, life-threatening illnesses, as well as the stress of work, a divorce, bankruptcy, the loss of my father, and the constant rejection that's a part of every freelance writer's life. I've lost count of how many times I've reached a point where going on with life seemed to take more effort than I had left.

Yet I still go on, not through my own effort, but through the Lord's. As Christians, we're taught to turn our struggles over to Him, but we are also human; we tend to try to take over again, pushing through life on our own skills and abilities. I know I do, even though I'm a walking example of how God can lift us up. I've often been down to my last few dollars; yet, every time I surrendered to Him, the phone would ring the next day with work. When my daughter struggled for breath and the doctors had given up, God gave her nurse and me new ideas for her care and the strength and help to implement them.

This time I had been praying about possibly going back to an office job, but I didn't know if I could find one that would work with my daughter's care-giving schedule. Finally, I turned it over to Him, and God opened some amazing doors. Within a week, I had a job offer from a company willing to work with me on Rachel's needs.

God, in His great wisdom, knows far more about what we need than we do. When we believe and trust, when we lean on His understanding, He will set our paths right before us.

CONFIDENCE IN HIS FORGIVING LOVE

The woman then left her waterpot, went her way
into the city, and said to the men,
"Come, see a Man who told me all things
that I ever did. Could this be the Christ?"
Then they went out of the city and came to Him.

JOHN 4:28–30 NKJV

This woman of Samaria must have been shocked to her very core when Jesus spoke to her. She expressed her surprise at His approach, asking how He could dare talk to her (verse 9). After all, she was a woman, a Samaritan, and an outcast, which gave this Jewish rabbi called Jesus three perfectly good reasons to turn His back on her.

She was used to being shunned. The Samaritans, despite their estrangement from the Jews, were a moral people who worshiped God (verse 20) and followed the Law of the Old Testament. She had broken that law by her immoral lifestyle, and the fact that she was filling her water pot in the heat of the day clearly indicated her avoidance of other people. Women normally drew water for their homes first thing in the morning, or in the cool of the evening, and these were times of community, sharing, and friendship. The other women of the town would have resisted associating with her, and possibly even ridiculed her.

Yet this man did not. He asked her for water—and about her life. He told her of His own living water, about a life without spiritual thirst. Jesus spoke bluntly to her about her past husbands, and that she now lived with a man without being married to him.

She may have been immoral, but this was one smart woman! She knew the scriptures, and she recognized Jesus as a prophet. When she spoke to Him about the coming Christ, He acknowledged that He was the One (verse 26).

Wouldn't you be excited? She certainly was! She immediately ran back into the city to spread the news. She didn't think about being ridiculed or avoided; she even forgot her water pot! She brought the whole city out to hear the news of the Messiah.

When Christ comes into our lives, whatever past sins may have clouded our lives are forgiven. Wiped clean. As with the Samaritan woman, He doesn't care what we were; only what we are going to be now that He is a part of us. We can start fresh, having the confidence to push forward and face whatever has been holding us back.

CONFIDENCE FROM HIS SACRIFICE

"This is My commandment, that you love one another as I have loved you. Greater love has no one than this, than to lay down one's life for his friends."

JOHN 15:12–13 NKJV

Throughout this book, a number of devotionals have focused on a personal confidence that is drawn from all the beautiful things God does for us. He cares for us and those we love; He answers our many prayers, great and small. He protects us and guides us, giving us a sweet refuge from the storms that rock our lives. When we are weak in mind, body, or spirit, His strength carries us through.

All this giving and love, however, is not just a one-way street. Or even a two-way street. He expects us—and in this verse commands us—to love each other. To send out that love in all directions. . . To treat each other the way He has treated us—with nurturing love, gentle correction, guidance along the way, and support when life sends us tumbling. Most of all, He provides us with the ultimate example of this commandment to love one another.

He died for us.

When God became incarnate as Jesus Christ, He continued to do in a physical form what He had already been doing spiritually. He walked among us, touched us, healed us, loved us. But He came here specifically to die for us, to make that sacrifice so that we no longer had to face death. Now we can live eternally with Him, if we choose to, if we believe.

And if we do believe, then we are drawing on the greatest power, the greatest love in the universe. The confidence that grows out of that knowledge can be boundless. We may not always succeed, and troubles may fill our paths, but the spirit—the confidence—to get up and strive on in His will comes from knowing one simple fact.

When you walk with God, nothing is impossible.

ABOUT THE AUTHOR

Ramona Richards is a freelance writer and editor living in Tennessee. Formerly the editor of *Ideals* magazine, Ramona has also edited children's books, fiction, nonfiction, study Bibles, and reference books for major Christian publishers. She is the author of *A Moment with God for Single Parents*.

ACKNOWLEDGMENTS

I'd like to thank all the women who shared their stories with me for this book, including those in my church and community as well those who have a global ministry. Special thanks go to Marcheta Berry, whose friendship, strength, and God-inspired confidence are unparalleled. She is a true inspiration.

If you'd like more information on the ministries of the women mentioned here, please check out these Web sites:

Carol Grace Anderson (getfiredup.com)

Allison Gappa Bottke (godallowsuturns.com)

Jan Eckles (janeckles.com)

Eva Marie Everson (evamarieeverson.com)

Shelley Hendrix (marys-vineyard.org)

Tracy Hurst (therobinsonagency.com)

Connie Neumann (connieneumann.com)

Ann Platz (annplatz.com)

Linda Evans Shepherd (righttotheheart.com)

Cheryl Wolverton (cherylwolverton.com)

Finally, I thank God for all He's done for me, including the confidence He gave me that I could, in fact, write this book.

RAMONA RICHARDS
www.ramonarichards.com

If you enjoyed

(SECRETS OF)
C*O*NFIDENCE

be sure to check out Rebecca Barlow Jordan's
title. . .also available from Barbour Publishing:

*D*AILY
IN YOUR
IMAGE

ISBN 1-59310-157-0

Available wherever Christian books are sold.